God . . . gives songs in the night.

Job 35:10

Also by Henry Gariepy

Names and Titles of Jesus
Footsteps to Calvary
Study Guide — Footsteps to Calvary
The Advent of Jesus Christ
Study Guide — The Advent of Jesus Christ
100 Portraits of Christ
Portraits of Perseverance
Christianity in Action
Wisdom to Live By
General of God's Army
Challenge and Response
40 Days with the Savior
A Light in a Dark Place
Guidebook for Writers and Editors
Healing in the Heartland

Songs in the Night

*Inspiring Stories behind 100 Hymns
Born in Trial and Suffering*

Henry Gariepy

WILLIAM B. EERDMANS PUBLISHING COMPANY
GRAND RAPIDS, MICHIGAN / CAMBRIDGE, U.K.

Printed in the United States of America

01 00 99 98 97 96   7 6 5 4 3 2

Library of Congress Cataloging-in-Publication Data

Gariepy, Henry.
    Songs in the night : inspiring stories behind 100 hymns
  born in trial and suffering / Henry Gariepy.
      p.   cm.
    ISBN 0-8028-3802-2 (cloth : alk. paper)
    1. Hymns, English — History and criticism.
    2. Hymns — Devotional use. I. Title.
  BV315.G37 1996
  264'.2 — dc20   95-51769
                                             CIP

The author and publisher gratefully acknowledge permission to reprint the text of hymns
granted by the individuals and institutions listed on p. 249.

To Kathy
To whom God has given
Songs in the Night

Contents

II SONGS OF PRAYER

V SONGS OF DEVOTION

VI SONGS OF TESTIMONY

XI SONGS OF HISTORY

Introduction

Ultimately, a "night season" will come into each life. These nights of doubt, of trial, of broken relationships, of loneliness, of anxiety, of misunderstanding, of bewilderment, of loss often will be a time of testing and trial.

It is easy to sing in the sunshine when life flows along like a song. But at night the song must emerge from the shadows and come from the melody that the Lord puts within one's life.

But the night has its songs as well. The song of the nightingale is sweeter because it comes in the stillness of the night. The noises of the day are hushed and her notes float as sweet music through the night air.

God is the great Composer of the night songs. When darkness overtakes us, God gives a song. This truth is enshrined in the hymn:

> *There is never a day so dreary,*
> *There is never a night so long,*
> *But the soul that is trusting Jesus,*
> *Will somewhere find a song.*

The Psalmist testified, "At night His song is with me" (42:8), and "I remembered my songs in the night" (77:6). In the midst of a crisis in Israel, God promised his people, "You shall have a song as in the night" (Isa. 30:29, NKJV). Out of the tragic story of Job's trials comes the radiant truth that "God . . . gives songs in the night" (Job 35:10). Sorrow becomes the expositor of the mysteries of God that joy leaves unexplained.

This radiant truth has been confirmed in the experience of innumerable people who, when going through the dark valleys, have been encouraged and sustained by the song God gave to them. Many of our best-loved hymns were born in the crucible of sorrow and suffering. An anonymous poet reminds us:

> Many a rapturous minstrel
> Among the sons of light,
> Will say of his sweetest music,
> "I learned it in the night."
> And many a rolling anthem
> That fills the Father's throne,
> Sobbed out its first rehearsal
> In the shade of a darkened room.

A Hasidic saying contends that a person expresses deep sorrow in three ways: The person on the lowest level cries; the person on the second level is silent; the person on the highest level knows how to turn the sorrow into song. In this book, *Songs in the Night*, we will see biblical, historical, and contemporary examples of those who turned their sorrows into songs.

The unique aspect of this book is that the selection of songs comes from those composed or used in the crucible of trial and sorrow. Charlotte Elliott wrote "Just As I Am" when she was a helpless invalid. Francis Ridley Havergal, author of "Take My Life" and many other hymns, suffered ill health. "God Moves in a Mysterious Way" was composed by William Cowper in an hour of mental distress. "What a Friend We Have in Jesus" was written by the young Joseph Scriven when not long before his wedding day his fiance was drowned. Fanny Crosby was blind all of her life and yet wrote over six thousand hymns, many of them among all-time favorites. Our most cherished hymns were often forged on the anvil of deep trial and sorrow. These stories that tell of the circumstances in which the songs were written, make them all the more a source of inspiration and blessing to us.

The words of Longfellow remind us of the ministry from this "Fifth Gospel According To the Hymns":

> God sent His singers upon the earth
> With songs of sadness and of mirth,
> That they might touch the hearts of men,
> And bring them back to Heaven again.

"There is no such raw material," wrote F. B. Meyer, "for songs that live from heart to heart as that furnished by sorrow." May these songs, and the stories behind them, resonate with a special blessing to our lives.

I SONGS OF FAITH

1 It Is Well with My Soul

A Song in the Storm

After the great Chicago fire of 1871, Horatio Spafford (1828–88), a Chicago lawyer, arranged an ocean voyage to Europe for his family, where he would join them later. The ship on which the happy family sailed, the *Ville du Havre*, never got farther than halfway across the Atlantic.

In the dead of the night, it was rammed by a sailing vessel and cut in two. In the confusion and disaster that followed, Mrs. Spafford saw her four daughters swept away to their deaths. A falling mast knocked her unconscious, and a wave freakishly deposited her body on a piece of wreckage where, later, she regained consciousness.

When she and a few other survivors reached Wales, she cabled two words to her husband: "Saved alone."

Taking the earliest ship, he hastened to his wife's side, all the ache of his heart going out to her and to his Father God. When his boat reached the approximate spot where the *Ville du Havre* had met with disaster, God gave him the inspiration and courage to write:

> *When peace like a river attendeth my way,*
> *When sorrows like sea-billows roll,*
> *Whatever my lot, Thou hast taught me to say:*
> *It is well, it is well with my soul.*
>
> *Though Satan should buffet, though trials should come,*
> *Let this blest assurance control,*

That Christ hath regarded my helpless estate,
And hath shed his own blood for my soul.

But Lord, 'tis for thee, for thy coming we wait,
The sky, not the grave, is our goal;
O trump of the angel! O voice of the Lord!
Blessed hope, blessed rest of my soul!

When the storms of life would overwhelm us, if we look to him, God has a song in the night for us — a song of strength, of peace, of hope. Let us listen and catch the strains that come from the Composer of songs for the night season of our soul.

2 He Giveth More Grace

Added Grace in Added Affliction

Annie Johnson Flint (1866–1932) has written some of the most inspiring poems dealing with faith and triumph in time of trial and suffering. It seemed that a personal experience of suffering or trial must be behind such writing. Research confirmed this supposition.

Born in Vineland, New Jersey, Annie Johnson lost both parents before she was six years of age. A childless couple named Flint adopted her. While still in her teens she became afflicted with arthritis and soon was unable even to walk.

She aspired to be a composer and concert pianist, but when illness deprived her of her ability to play the piano she resorted to writing poetry. She set several of her poems to music. In later life, being unable to open her hands, she wrote many of her poems on the typewriter, using but her knuckles.

Out of her own deep affliction has come one of the songs that has blessed an innumerable company in time of suffering or trial — "He Giveth More Grace." The author based her words on three Bible promises in the Authorized Version: "He giveth more grace" (Jas. 4:6); "He increaseth strength" (Isa. 40:29); and "Mercy unto you, and peace, and love, be multiplied" (Jude 2).

> *He giveth more grace as our burdens grow greater,*
> *He sendeth more strength as our labors increase,*
> *To added afflictions He addeth his mercy,*
> *To multiplied trials He multiplies peace.*

When we have exhausted our store of endurance,
When our strength has failed ere the day is half-done,
When we reach the end of our hoarded resources
Our Father's full giving is only begun.

His love has no limits, His grace has no measure,
His power no boundary known unto men;
For out of His infinite riches in Jesus
He giveth, and giveth, and giveth again.

There is a grace and strength from God that is not given in the everyday routine of life. But God gives it to us in our hour of need when our trust is in him. When troubles and trials come upon us, may we know his added grace, his increased strength, and his multiplied peace.

3 His Eye Is on the Sparrow

An Invalid's Secret of Joy

We all are at some time tempted to be discouraged. Circumstance, sorrow, or trial come upon us and in our humanness we can lose the joy and courage that should be ours.

The hymn "His Eye Is on the Sparrow" was inspired by a couple, the Doolittles of Elmira, New York, who had reason to be discouraged. For twenty years Mrs. Doolittle had been confined to bed as an invalid. Her husband, a partial invalid, managed his business from a wheelchair.

One day, the evangelist Dr. W. Stillman Martin and his wife came to visit them. Together they had written the beautiful hymn "God Will Take Care of You," with Mrs. Martin writing the words and Dr. Martin the music.

The Martins were deeply impressed with the joyful spirit that the Doolittles maintained in spite of severe adversity. "What is the secret of your joy?" Dr. Martin asked. "His eye is on the sparrow," Mrs. Doolittle replied, "and I know he watches me."

That reply lodged in the mind and soul of Mrs. Martin, who pondered the questions and answers Mrs. Doolittle's testimony had inspired, and set them to the verses that today are so well known.

> *Why should I feel discouraged?*
> *Why should the shadows come?*
> *Why should my heart feel lonely,*
> *And long for Heaven and home,*
> *When Jesus is my portion?*
> *My constant Friend is He;*

> His eye is on the sparrow,
> And I know He watches me;
>
> "Let not your heart be troubled,"
> His tender Word I heard,
> And resting on His goodness,
> I lose my doubts and fears;
> Tho' by the path He leadeth
> But one step I may see;
> His eye is on the sparrow,
> And I know He watches me.

Many of us will forever associate this song with the beloved African-American blues singer and actress, Ethel Waters. She had been converted at the age of twelve. When in 1957 she walked into Madison Square Garden to attend a Billy Graham Crusade meeting, she "felt that my Lord was calling me back home." Ethel joined the chorus of 1,500 and sang at each service to secure a reserved seat for the eight weeks of the crusade. "So many things I had pondered about for a lifetime," she later witnessed, "the Lord cleared up during these weeks."

Cliff Barrows, the crusade choir leader, learned of her presence when she signed a choir petition for the extension of the crusade. Asked to sing a solo, she sang "His Eye Is on the Sparrow." For five nights in the final weeks of the crusade Ethel Waters sang that song. The experience changed her life. She testified, "I found that I could no longer act every role I was offered and continue to glorify my Lord."

Ethel Waters attended crusades year by year, at her own expense, to sing this song in her inimitable style. It became one of the hallmarks of the Billy Graham crusades.

May the joyful chorus of this song, inspired by an invalid couple, composed by two servants of God, and made famous by a blues singer at Billy Graham crusades, be our daily experience:

> I sing because I'm happy,
> I sing because I'm free,
> For His eye is on the sparrow,
> And I know he watches me.

4 What a Friend We Have in Jesus

Comfort for a Sick and Distant Mother

Joseph Scriven (1819–86) discovered early in life how much he needed the presence of Christ. Born in Ireland, he looked forward to a blissful life with the Irish lass of his choice. But then tragedy struck. On the eve of his intended wedding day, his bride-to-be was accidentally drowned.

In his loneliness and sorrow, he left the Emerald Isle and emigrated to Canada at the age of twenty-five. Once again he became engaged to be married, only to lose his second fiancée after a brief but fatal illness.

He knew the pain of loneliness, the pinch of poverty, and concern for his own precarious health. Yet he spent the rest of his life helping the physically handicapped and underprivileged. He often shared his food with the needy and even gave them his clothes.

But his good deeds and the story of his life would never have been known by Christendom had not Joseph Scriven written twenty-four lines to comfort his mother during a time of serious illness. It had been ten years since he had kissed her goodbye and he now was unable to go to her side. He wrote a poem and sent it with the prayer that it would remind her of her never-failing friend, Jesus.

Scriven's immortal lines lay dormant until sometime later the words appeared in a publication that was eventually seen by a German-American lawyer and composer, Charles Converse. His simple, inspiring tune gave the wings of melody to Scriven's three verses that would send it around the world.

That private message, written to comfort a sick and distant mother, has become a beloved hymn of comfort and assurance to millions of Christians around the world. It was listed as the fifth most popular hymn in a 1990 newspaper national poll.

> What a Friend we have in Jesus
>   All our sins and griefs to bear;
> What a privilege to carry
>   Everything to God in prayer.
> O what peace we often forfeit,
>   O what needless pain we bear;
> All because we do not carry
>   Everything to God in prayer.
>
> Have we trials and temptations?
>   Is there trouble anywhere?
> We should never be discouraged;
>   Take it to the Lord in prayer.
> Can we find a friend so faithful
>   Who will all our sorrows share?
> Jesus knows our every weakness;
>   Take it to the Lord in prayer.
>
> Are we weak and heavy-laden,
>   Cumbered with a load of care?
> Precious Savior, still our refuge —
>   Take it to the Lord in prayer.
> Do thy friends despise, forsake thee?
>   Take it to the Lord in prayer;
> In His arms He'll take and shield thee,
>   Thou wilt find a solace there.

5 Peace, Perfect Peace

Composed at the Bedside
of a Dying Relative

Is it possible to have peace in "this dark world of sin," when we are "by thronging duties pressed," buffeted "with sorrows surging round," with "loved ones far away," haunted by forebodings of "our future all unknown"?

These five probing questions that pose challenges to our faith come from the first line of each verse of the hymn, "Peace, Perfect Peace." The hymn also gives the comforting answer to each of these imposing questions. Most of us can relate to one or more of these difficult life situations and take comfort in the answer given.

Edward Bickersteth (1825–1906), author of the hymn, was a minister of the Anglican Church in England and author of twelve volumes of prose and poetry. While vacationing in England, he heard a sermon that had a profound impact on him. His colleague preached on the text, "Thou wilt keep him in perfect peace whose mind is stayed on Thee" (Isa. 26:3). The preacher said that the original Hebrew version of this text reads, "Thou wilt keep him in peace peace whose mind is stayed on Thee," and explained that the repetition in the Hebrew conveys the idea of absolute perfection. The translators of the King James Version knew of this Hebrew method and instead of repeating the word *peace*, which would seem awkward, translated it to "perfect peace" so that all could understand the meaning of the text.

That very afternoon Bickersteth visited an aged and dying relative. He found the man in deep depression and troubled about his impending death. To comfort him he read the Isaiah text still fresh in his mind. When his friend dropped off to sleep he took a sheet of paper and began to write a poem, posing the most disturbing obstacles to peace in life and then answering with an affirmation of faith that could not be denied. When the patient awoke, the author read the stanzas to him and comfort came to his troubled mind and heart.

It is said that these lines have remained unchanged since composed by the bedside of the dying man. These words of comfort to a dying loved one as he slipped into eternity continue to bring assurance to troubled hearts today.

Later his hymn would comfort his own heart as he stood over the grave of a preacher son. The message of this hymn has brought comfort to many hearts and affirms what each of us need to know.

> *Peace, perfect peace — in this dark world of sin?*
> *The blood of Jesus whispers peace within.*

> *Peace, perfect peace — by thronging duties pressed?*
> *To do the will of Jesus, this is rest.*

> *Peace, perfect peace — with sorrows surging round?*
> *On Jesus' bosom naught but calm is found.*

> *Peace, perfect peace — with loved ones far away?*
> *In Jesus' keeping we are safe, and they.*

> *Peace, perfect peace — our future all unknown?*
> *Jesus we know, and He is on the throne.*

The composer answers each challenge with an affirmation in Christ. What is it that may rob us of our peace? Is it sin that wrecks our peace? If so, the atonement, the blood of Christ, is the answer. Is it the pressure of work? Then let us conform to his will. Is it sorrow? Christ is the source of comfort. Is it separation? Trust your loved one to him. Is it the unknown future? Trust the ruler of the universe. Is death staring you in the face? Trust the Risen Lord.

Christ not only has the answer to our need of peace, but "He Himself is our peace!" (Eph. 2:14). Claim the precious promises of his word and "let the peace of Christ rule in your hearts" (Col. 3:15).

6 Joni's Song

A Song from a Wheelchair

One of the most radiant persons I have ever met is Joni Eareckson Tada. She effervesces with praise to the Lord. Yet Joni would seem to have good reason not to live a life of praise.

A quadriplegic — paralyzed from the shoulders down from a diving accident at the age of seventeen — she says, "God has used my wheelchair to change me and make me more like Him."

"I learned long ago," she testifies, "that God's purpose in redeeming us is not to primarily make our lives happy, healthy or free from trouble. God's purpose in redeeming us is to make us more like Jesus."

Her far-reaching world ministry includes over a half-dozen books that have sold in the millions, a daily radio program, several recordings, and the starring role in the movie about her life. She is a popular and compelling speaker and now directs Joni and Friends — a program working with churches in ministry to those with handicaps.

Joni shares a vibrant witness: "My paralysis has drawn me close to God and given a spiritual healing which I wouldn't trade for a hundred active years on my feet. God's grace enables me to rejoice, not in spite of my disability, but because of my disability . . . God has a way of reaching down and wrenching good out of it. God aborted Satan's scheme in my life and brought positive good out of it."

The Lord has given Joni a number of "songs in the night" that, through her recordings, have inspired many. She describes one such experience: "In one of those mad, midnight moments during my long convalescence, I came up with a song. Since I couldn't jump out of bed and get a pad of paper and pen, I carefully pondered and memorized each phrase as it came. When the whole poem was complete in my head, I didn't feel so depressed about the will of God." The following is the song God gave to her in that night season of her soul.

I have a piece of china,
A pretty porcelain vase.
It holds such lovely flowers,
Captures everybody's gaze.
But fragile things do slip and fall
As everybody knows,
And when that vase came crashing down,
Those tears began to flow.

My life was just like china,
A lovely thing to me.
Full of porcelain promises
Of all that I might be.
But fragile things do slip and fall
As everybody knows,
And when my life came crashing down,
Those tears began to flow.

Now Jesus is no porcelain prince,
His promises won't break.
His holy Word holds fast and sure,
His love no one can shake.
So if your life is shattered
By sorrow, pain, or sin,
His healing love will reach right down
And make you whole again.

Joni's beautiful "song in the night" speaks to all of us in times "when pretty things get broken."

7 'Tis So Sweet to Trust in Jesus

From a Husband's Tragic Drowning

Louisa Stead (1850–1917), her husband, and their four-year-old daughter Lily went to enjoy a sunny day on the beach on Long Island Sound. While they were having their picnic lunch, they suddenly heard cries of help and spotted a drowning boy in the sea. Mr. Stead rushed to rescue the boy but, as often happens, the struggling and terrified child pulled his rescuer under the water with him. Both drowned as his horrified wife and daughter watched helplessly.

Louisa Stead struggled with the question of why her husband, who with her was committed to serving Christ, should lose his life in such a tragedy, leaving her and her daughter bereft and all of the promise of his life lost. She surrendered her doubts and despair and, in this dark hour of her life, composed the words that have been a comfort to many in times of stress and loss:

> 'Tis so sweet to trust in Jesus,
> Just to take Him at His word,
> Just to rest upon His promise,
> Just to know, "Thus saith the Lord."
>
> Jesus, Jesus, How I trust Him!
> How I've proved Him o'er and o'er!
> Jesus, Jesus, precious Jesus!
> O for grace to trust Him more!

> *Yes, 'tis sweet to trust in Jesus,*
> *Just from sin and self to cease,*
> *Just from Jesus simply taking*
> *Life and rest and joy and peace.*

> *I'm so glad I learned to trust Thee,*
> *Precious Jesus, Savior, Friend;*
> *And I know that Thou art with me,*
> *Wilt be with me to the end.*

In the tragic drowning of her husband, a young wife and mother affirmed through her tears that there is comfort and grace in Christ. Louisa Stead, soon after the tragedy, went with her daughter to serve faithfully for twenty-five years as a missionary in South Africa and Southern Rhodesia. Her missionary comrades in Southern Rhodesia wrote this tribute after her death: "Her influence goes on as our five thousand native Christians continually sing her hymn in their native language."

We too may be called upon to enter the bleak deserts of barrenness or the dark canyons of anguish. In such times we can also know the peace that comes through trust in the Savior and go on to fruitful service for him. Trust will bring triumph. May we in our sunlit days, as well as in our darkest hours, know the sweetness, the serenity, and the strength that comes when we trust in Jesus.

8 My Faith Looks Up to Thee

In a Time of Illness and Loneliness

Ray Palmer (1808–87) experienced hardship early in life, having to leave school at the age of thirteen to work in a dry-goods store in Boston. He soon thereafter came to faith in Christ. His faith led him later to complete school, graduate from Yale, and go on to the ministry.

Following his studies he was overcome with illness and loneliness. At the age of twenty-one, in the midst of despair, he sought comfort by writing a poem. His composition came as a spontaneous expression of a deep inner experience of the presence of Christ and a realization of what Christ meant to him and to the world.

Palmer had no idea that his words would be used as a hymn. But the poem was brought to the attention of Lowell Mason, one of America's great hymn-tune composers. He wedded the words to the now familiar tune *Olivet,* sending Palmer's poem around the world to become one of Christendom's great hymns.

The hymn is a prayer of faith. It acknowledges Christ as our Savior and source of grace and inspiration. It petitions the Lord's cleansing, strengthening, guidance, and comfort. The words also voice our prayer for a pure and changeless love, and to be kept faithful.

> *My faith looks up to thee,*
> *Thou Lamb of Calvary,*
> *Savior divine;*
> *Now hear me while I pray,*
> *Take all my guilt away,*

17

O let me from this day
  Be wholly thine!

May thy rich grace impart
Strength to my fainting heart,
  My zeal inspire;
As thou hast died for me,
O may my love to thee
Pure, warm and changeless be,
  A living fire!

While life's dark maze I tread,
And griefs around me spread,
  Be thou my guide;
Bid darkness turn to day,
Wipe sorrow's tears away,
Nor let me ever stray
  From thee aside.

We all have embarked on a pilgrimage that will bring unknown testings, and perhaps trials. Let us reaffirm our faith in Christ and lean on his grace and guidance.

9 I Must Tell Jesus

An Answer to a Heart Cry

Elisha A. Hoffman (1839–1929), an evangelical pastor, wrote almost two thousand gospel hymns, including, "Are You Washed in the Blood?," "Leaning on the Everlasting Arms," and "Glory to His Name." He tells how he came to write the words of one of his most popular hymns, "I Must Tell Jesus."

"There was a woman to whom God permitted many visitations of sorrow and affliction. Coming to her home one day, I found her much discouraged. She unburdened her heart, concluding with the question, 'Brother Hoffman, what shall I do? What shall I do?' I quoted from the word, then added, 'You cannot do better than to take all of your sorrows to Jesus. You must tell Jesus.'"

"For a moment she seemed lost in meditation. Then her eyes lighted as she exclaimed, 'Yes, I must tell Jesus.' As I left her home I had a vision of that joy-illuminated face . . . and I heard all along my pathway the echo, "I must tell Jesus. I must tell Jesus."

When pastor Hoffman reached his study he penned the words, and a short time later the melody, for what has become the popular gospel song.

I must tell Jesus all of my trials,
I cannot bear these burdens alone;
In my distress He kindly will help me,
He ever loves and cares for His own.

I must tell Jesus! I must tell Jesus!
I cannot bear my burdens alone;
I must tell Jesus! I must tell Jesus!
Jesus can help me, Jesus alone.

I must tell Jesus all of my troubles,
He is a kind, compassionate Friend;
If I but ask Him, He will deliver,
Make of my troubles quickly an end.

Tempted and tried, I need a great Savior,
One who can help my burdens to bear;
I must tell Jesus, I must tell Jesus,
He all my cares and sorrows will share.

When our life is overtaken by trial, how helpful it is to be able to talk to a friend, one who will listen, who will be a source of understanding and strength. Jesus invites us to bring our burdens to Him: "Come to me, all you who are weary and burdened, and I will give you rest" (Matt. 11:28).

Are you beset with sorrow or anxiety? The counsel of the wise pastor to the heart cry of his parishioner in her dark night of the soul is one for all of us to heed. Too often we try to carry our burdens ourselves, to work things out with our own limited resources. We tend to forget the gracious and great invitation of God's word: "Cast all your anxiety on Him because He cares for you" (1 Pet. 5:7).

How assuring that we can take our troubles to the Lord and find in him One who cares and understands. Today, take your burden to the Lord in prayer, and find his guidance, power, and peace.

10 Leaning on the Everlasting Arms

Comfort for the Grief-Stricken

Minister and music teacher Anthony Showalter received letters from two men in 1888 who had attended a music school he had conducted just a few weeks before. The letters conveyed the tragic news that their wives had died.

As he thought about what he might say as a word of comfort to these grief-stricken men, the great Bible promise came to his mind: "The eternal God is your refuge, and underneath are the everlasting arms" (Deut. 33:27). Inspired by this verse, he composed a melody and the refrain:

> *Leaning, leaning,*
> *Safe and secure from all alarms;*
> *Leaning, leaning,*
> *Leaning on the everlasting arms.*

Unable to complete the stanzas for the hymn, he sent the music and chorus to Elisha Hoffman, a well-known hymn writer, asking him to supply the needed stanzas. Mr. Hoffman wrote the stanzas, which with the melody and chorus have been a blessing and comfort to many.

> *What a fellowship, what a joy divine,*
> *Leaning on the everlasting arms;*
> *What a blessedness, what a peace is mine,*
> *Leaning on the everlasting arms.*

> *O how sweet to walk in this pilgrim way;*
> *Leaning on the everlasting arms;*
> *O how bright the path grows from day to day,*
> *Leaning on the everlasting arms.*
>
> *What have I to dread, what have I to fear,*
> *Leaning on the everlasting arms?*
> *I have blessed peace with my Lord so near,*
> *Leaning on the everlasting arms.*

Are you burdened with a grief or sorrow? Then let the wonderful Bible promise that inspired this hymn comfort your heart with its message of assurance.

It is no less than the eternal God who is your refuge. In Scripture, the arm is the symbol of power. The mighty arms of the Lord will uphold and sustain you in your hour of need. Claim God's promise and lean on those everlasting arms.

11 Rock of Ages

In the Fury of a Storm

Augustus Toplady, born in 1740, was converted in a barn in an Irish village at age sixteen after listening to a sermon. He became a minister and editor of *The Gospel* magazine.

Toplady was in a field in England in 1776 when suddenly a violent storm broke out. He was far from town and shelter, but saw a large rock and hurried to it to try to find some break from the brunt of the storm's fury. In the rock he found a crack into which he could fit. He entered it and was sheltered.

While waiting out the storm Toplady reflected how Christ, who is called our Rock of Salvation, was broken that we might find in him shelter from the coming judgment. On a playing card he found at his feet, he wrote the poem that begins with the words, "Rock of Ages, cleft for me, let me hide myself in thee."

This renowned hymn, born in the fury of a storm, eloquently voices our prayer for God's salvation and security for the believer. May it be the petition of our heart.

> *Rock of ages, cleft for me,*
> *Let me hide myself in Thee;*
> *Let the water and the Blood,*
> *From Thy riven side which flowed,*
> *Be of sin the double cure,*
> *Cleanse me from its guilt and power.*

Not the labors of my hands
Can fulfil Thy law's demands;
Could my zeal no respite know,
Could my tears for ever flow,
All for sin could not atone;
Thou must save, and Thou alone.

Nothing in my hand I bring,
Simply to Thy Cross I cling;
Naked, come to Thee for dress,
Helpless, look to Thee for grace,
Foul, I to the fountain fly;
Wash me, Savior, or I die.

While I draw this fleeting breath,
When mine eyes shall close in death,
When I soar to worlds unknown,
See Thee on Thy judgment throne,
Rock of ages, cleft for me,
Let me hide myself in Thee.

12 God Will Take Care of You

Born upon a Bed of Affliction

Civilla D. Martin (1869–1948) was confined to a sickbed. Unable to leave the house, she composed the words of a song one Sunday afternoon in 1904 that expressed her faith amid trial. When she showed her husband the words after he returned from a preaching mission, he sat down at a pump organ in their home and composed the tune — appropriately called *Martin*.

This hymn, born upon a bed of affliction, became a source of comfort for many who bear the burdens of illness and hardship.

> *Be not dismayed whate'er betide,*
> *God will take care of you;*
> *Beneath His wings of love abide,*
> *God will take care of you.*

> *God will take care of you,*
> *Through every day, o'er all the way;*
> *He will take care of you,*
> *God will take care of you.*

> *Through days of toil when heart doth fail,*
> *God will take care of you;*
> *When dangers fierce your path assail,*
> *God will take care of you.*

All you may need He will provide,
God will take care of you;
Nothing you ask will be denied,
God will take care of you.

Misfortune and hardship are the rule, not the exception, of life. Job's famous epigram reminds us that "man is born to trouble" (Job 5:7). But just as an eagle uses the wind and storm to reach greater heights, so the child of God, on wings of faith, rises above life's hardships to new heights of strength and holiness.

The now familiar story is told of a man who dreamed that he was reviewing with the Lord scenes of his life portrayed as footprints along a sandy beach. Usually there were two sets of footprints — his and the Lord's. But as he looked closer, he noted only one set of footprints along the very rugged places, where suffering, sorrow, or defeat prevailed.

He said to the Lord, "You promised me that if I followed you, you would walk with me always. But I have noticed that during the most trying periods of my life there has been only one set of footprints in the sand. Why, when I needed you most, have you not been there for me?"

The Lord replied, "My child, I have never left you. When you came to those perilous times when it was almost more than you could bear, I carried you in my arms. When you have seen only one set of footprints I carried you."

We may be tempted to feel alone, forsaken, and forgotten. But let us remember that the Lord is with us always. God does not promise that he will deliver us from trial but he promises that he will give grace that will carry us through.

So, "be not dismayed whate'er betide"; be assured that "God will take care of you."

13 Blest Be the Tie That Binds

A Sadness of Farewell

After serving a small rural pastorate for seven years John Fawcett recorded in his diary: "During these years our family has increased faster than our income." When a few weeks later in 1772 a call came from a famous Baptist Church in London it seemed like an answer to prayer. The move from an impoverished congregation to a larger and more prosperous church would benefit the family in many ways. The future looked promising for the thirty-two-year-old Fawcett as he and his family prepared to make the transition.

The Fawcetts had become an integral part of the life of their Yorkshire village, and deep friendships were forged. On the day of departure, Fawcett preached his final sermon, said his good-byes, and loaded the family's belongings into a horse-drawn wagon. As he, his wife, and their children were saying their final farewells, they saw the tear-stained faces of their friends. So moved was Fawcett by the deep love of his parishioners that he made a life-changing decision. He gave the order to unload his household goods, and stayed on in their small home and pastorate.

The following Sunday, John Fawcett preached from the text that says, "A man's life does not consist in the abundance of his possessions (Luke 12:15). At the close of the sermon, he read a poem he had composed, entitled "Brotherly Love." Years later the verses were set to music to become one of our most famous and well-loved hymns. Had John Fawcett gone on to the lure of bigger things in London, we would never have the blessing of singing:

Blest be the tie that binds
Our hearts in Christian love!
The fellowship of kindred minds
Is like to that above.

Before our Father's throne
We pour our ardent prayers;
Our fears, hopes, our aims are one,
Our comforts and our cares.

We share our mutual woes,
Our mutual burdens bear;
And often for each other flows
The sympathizing tear.

When we asunder part
It gives us inward pain;
But we shall still be joined in heart,
And hope to meet again.

Later Fawcett turned down a call to become the president of an academy. He was also honored by King George III. Remaining faithful as pastor for fifty-four years to his little flock, from that rural pastorate he wrote several books and 166 hymns, and started a boarding school to train preachers. He was remembered and loved for the example he set in sacrificing ambition and personal gain for devotion to the people God called him to serve.

With Tennyson's Ulysses we are all constrained to say, "I am a part of all that I have met." Relationships bring to us our highest enrichment, growth, fulfillment, and blessing. Our lives become immeasurably enriched by the love and encouragement of others. As children of our heavenly Father, we are blessed by "the tie that binds our hearts in Christian love." Bonded by the cords of love, we are strengthened to stand triumphant before life's testings and trials.

We too will come to the sadness of farewell within "the fellowship of kindred minds," and the parting of ways with loved ones. But as the poet preacher reminds us, "We shall still be joined in heart/And hope to meet again." If not in this life, then in the next!

II SONGS OF PRAYER

14 Lead, Kindly Light

In Gloom upon the High Seas

The words of one of our immortal hymns, "Lead, Kindly Light," emerged from John Henry Newman's struggle with depression and danger upon the high seas.

Newman was a leading influence in the religious life of nineteenth-century England. But in his early years his pace and spiritual struggles took a heavy toll, and he traveled to Italy for rest and recuperation. There he was stricken with a serious fever. Further depressed, he boarded a ship to return to his native England.

Sailing vessels in those days were dependent on the wind. Sailing on the Mediterranean Sea, the ship suddenly was becalmed. Sails hung limp on the masts. Not a breeze stirred for a week. Sick and depressed, closed in by the fog, faced with the prospect of starving at sea, he was led to write this prayer poem, pleading for God's guidance. He had no thought of it ever being used as a hymn.

But the Reverend John Dykes, composer of over three hundred hymn tunes, read Newman's poem in a magazine and composed the tune that gave wings to the words, establishing it as one of the great hymns of the Christian faith.

> Lead, kindly Light, amid the encircling gloom,
>   Lead Thou me on;
> The night is dark, and I am far from home,
>   Lead Thou me on.
> Keep Thou my feet; I do not ask to see

The distant scene —
One step enough for me.

I was not ever thus, nor prayed that
Thou shouldst lead me on;
I loved to choose and see my path; but now
Lead Thou me on.
I loved the garish day, and, spite of fears,
Pride ruled my will:
Remember not past years.

So long Thy power hath blest me, sure it still
Will lead me on,
O'er moor and fen, o'er crag and torrent, till
The night is gone;
And with the morn those angel faces smile,
Which I have loved long since,
And lost awhile.

Do you feel that life is closing in upon you? Is your life enshrouded by some fog of doubt or danger? Do you need guidance and power to find a way out? Perhaps, as Newman, you feel overcome with an "encircling gloom" and for you "the night is dark."

If so, make Newman's prayer — composed far from home during a time of depression and danger — your prayer to the One who came to be the Light of the world. And you too may find, not the "distant scene," but "one step enough for me."

15 O Master, Let Me Walk with Thee

Attacking Social Injustice

Following the Civil War, America was in the throes of the great industrial revolution. The poor were exploited for "economic progress." Washington Gladden (1836–1918) strongly believed in the social implications of the gospel and became a champion for social justice.

Gladden became a national figure by opposing New York City's notoriously corrupt Tweed Ring. His trenchant editorials as the religion editor for the influential *New York Independent* started the prosecution that sent the Tammany Hall boss, William Tweed, to prison for swindling public funds. As a pastor in Springfield, Massachusetts, Gladden preached on labor-management problems, and was one of the first in America to link the gospel with social implications for the poor.

He later moved to Columbus, Ohio, where he pastored a church for thirty-two years. There he became not only one of the most powerful pulpit voices in America but pioneered the application of the gospel to the social, economic, and political needs of the people.

Gladden was also active in arbitrating strikes and disputes. He believed and practiced that it was the duty of the Christian church to "elevate the masses not only spiritually and morally, but to be concerned about their social and economic welfare as well."

A contemporary of William Booth, Gladden shared in the belief that the gospel applied to the total person. Booth believed that the gospel should not only liberate one's soul from sin but also one's body and mind from the deprivation of poverty and social injustice.

When The Salvation Army's international leader, General Eva Burrows, was elected in 1986 she was asked, "What will be your position on political issues?" She replied, "While I definitely feel that the Army should have no partisan bias, I believe we should feel strongly about social injustice. If political means speaking out on issues such as prostitution or abortion, poverty and homelessness, if political means speaking out to quicken the conscience of the government on the needs of the people, then I'm political."

In America, Gladden is remembered with Walter Rauschenbush as the outstanding clergyman of his generation for applying the gospel to social issues. Gladden's concern for the poor and destitute led him in 1879 to pen his immortal prayer to walk with the Master "in lowly paths of service free" and to "bear the strain of toil, the fret of care."

> O Master, let me walk with Thee
> In lowly paths of service free;
> Tell me Thy secret, help me bear
> The strain of toil, the fret of care.
>
> Help me the slow of heart to move
> By some clear, winning word of love,
> Teach me the wayward feet to stay
> And guide them in the homeward way.
>
> Teach me Thy patience! Still with Thee
> In closer, dearer company,
> In work that keeps faith sweet and strong,
> In trust that triumphs over wrong.
>
> In hope that sends a shining ray
> Far down the future's broad'ning way,
> In peace that only Thou canst give,
> With Thee, O Master, let me live.

Indeed, our Christian faith should result in a compassion in action for those who suffer. We are called not to ivory towers of retreat from the world but to serve, out where the air is blowing, where the issues are real and where people are hurting.

16 Dear Lord and Father
of Mankind

Prayer for Sanity and Serenity

Slavery was one of the worst evils ever perpetrated by humankind. John Greenleaf Whittier, the Quaker poet (1807–92), used his pen without restraint against this monstrous evil. An ardent abolitionist, he joined the antislavery cause of his time. Britannica says of him: "Although a Quaker he had a polemical spirit and maintained his warfare against the national crime, employing action, argument, and lyric scorn." He wrote articles continuously and at one time was stoned by a mob.

Whittier's poetry and hymns reflect an unusual spiritual depth and insight. He was born and reared in the New England countryside. His schooling ended before the middle grades. Yet he left upon our literature the stamp of genius and upon our faith the touch of sanctity.

Whittier himself writes of his works: "They were written with no expectation that they would survive the occasions which called them forth. They were protests, alarm signals, trumpet-calls to action, words wrung from the writer's heart, forged at white heat."

He sought to show that Christ is not found in human systems, symbols, theologies, cathedrals, learned tomes, or in the Eucharist, but only in the human heart through faith and obedience.

In protest against the busyness and confusion of his world and the frenzied rituals and foolish rites of his day, he penned the stanzas that are among the most pure and beautiful hymns of Christendom. Its imagery is taken from the Bible.

In our fast-paced and confused world, more than ever we need the stillness and the quiet spaces of time to which these words call us.

Dear Lord and Father of mankind,
Forgive our foolish ways;
Reclothe us in our rightful mind;
In purer lives thy service find,
In deeper reverence, praise.

In simple trust like theirs who heard,
Beside the Syrian sea,
The gracious calling of the Lord,
Let us, like them, without a word
Rise up and follow thee.

O Sabbath rest by Galilee!
O calm of hills above,
Where Jesus knelt to share with thee
The silence of eternity,
Interpreted by love!

Drop thy still dews of quietness
Till all our strivings cease;
Take from our souls the strain and stress,
And let our ordered lives confess
The beauty of thy peace.

Breathe through the heats of our desire
Thy coolness and thy balm;
Let sense be dumb, let flesh retire;
Speak through the earthquake, wind and fire,
O still small voice of calm!

Another New Englander, Henry David Thoreau, also writing over a century ago, said of his age, "The mass of men lead lives of quiet desperation." Sadly, that diagnosis is more true today than ever. Our era of violence, terrorism, mass slaughters, and the ominous threat of nuclear holocaust, needs just such a trumpet-call as this hymn for sanity and sanctity.

Let this hymn, born out of the poet's protest, express our longing for God's presence and peace within our souls. We too need forgiveness for "foolish ways." We too need "purer lives" and "deeper reverence." We too need "the beauty of His peace" to replace our "strivings, strain and stress."

May we find these blessings in the quietness of prayer and in "the secret of His presence."

17 Sweet Hour of Prayer

A Song Carved in the Darkness

William Walford was an obscure lay preacher who owned a small novelty shop in the village of Coleshill, England. Although he had seen many "seasons of distress and grief," his optimism and bright spirit always uplifted those who visited his shop.

One day in 1842 a minister, Thomas Salmon, stopped in Walford's shop and found his friend had more on his mind that day than his usual carving. He had composed a poem and asked Rev. Salmon to take the words down as he recited them.

Three years later Salmon visited the United States and showed the old carver's poem to the editor of the *New York Observer*. The poem was first published in the September 13, 1845, issue. Then, fourteen years later, in 1859, a copy of it came to the attention of the noted composer of early gospel music, William Bradbury. He saw in Walford's poem material for a hymn, set it to music and published it. Borne on the wings of Bradbury's melody, the verse was soon sung around the world.

The reason William Walford had asked Rev. Salmon to take down his poem while he dictated it was because the old carver was blind. But in his night of physical darkness God gave a song that has brought comfort to an innumerable company.

Walford's familiar and beloved hymn reminds us of how sweet and precious is our hour of communion with God in prayer. No matter how dark and difficult our days, our heavenly Father bids us to "cast on Him our every care" and know the blessings and "fruits of the sweet hour of prayer." God inspired the composer to anticipate for everyone the day when faith will give way to sight.

This great hymn also calls us to spend more than a few hurried minutes in prayer, so we can know the rich blessing that comes in spending time in the presence of God. It is the best investment we will ever make for our soul and total life.

> *Sweet hour of prayer, sweet hour of prayer,*
> *That calls me from a world of care,*
> *And bids me at my Father's throne*
> *Make all my wants and wishes known;*
> *In seasons of distress and grief*
> *My soul has often found relief,*
> *And oft escaped the tempter's snare*
> *By thy return, sweet hour of prayer.*
>
> *Sweet hour of prayer, sweet hour of prayer,*
> *Thy wings shall my petition bear*
> *To Him whose truth and faithfulness*
> *Engage the waiting soul to bless;*
> *And since He bids me seek His face,*
> *Believe His word, and trust His grace,*
> *I'll cast on Him my every care*
> *And wait for Thee, sweet hour of prayer.*
>
> *Sweet hour of prayer, sweet hour of prayer,*
> *May I thy consolation share,*
> *Till from Mount Pisgah's lofty height*
> *I view my home, and at the sight*
> *Put off this robe of flesh, and rise*
> *To gain the everlasting prize,*
> *And realize for ever there*
> *The fruits of the sweet hour of prayer.*

18 I Need Thee Every Hour

God's Prevenient Grace

Often the Lord through some experience prepares us for a test or trial yet to come. Such was true of Annie S. Hawks (1835–1919), when as a young busy housewife and mother she was led to pen the words of the hymn, "I Need Thee Every Hour."

She records her experience in writing the words:

One day as a young wife and mother of 37 years of age, I was busy with my regular household tasks. Suddenly, I became filled with the sense of nearness to the Master, and I began to wonder how anyone could ever live without Him, either in joy or pain. Then the words were ushered into my mind and these thoughts took full possession of me.

Not until sixteen years later, with the death of her husband, did the full impact of these words minister to her own heart. She then wrote:

I did not understand at first why this hymn had touched the great throbbing heart of humanity. It was not until long after, when the shadow fell over my way, the shadow of a great loss, that I understood something of the comforting power in the words which I had been permitted to give out to others in my hour of sweet serenity and peace.

To be saved and filled with the Spirit does not bring in a charmed life, free of troubles and trial. "Each individual misfortune, to be sure, seems an exceptional occurrence," wrote Schopenhauer, "but misfortune in general is the rule."

Victor Frankl echoes this truth: "Suffering is an ineradicable part of life." Surely testings and trials will come to every life. When we are faithful today, God will prepare us for our troubles tomorrow.

Annie Hawks and her story reminds us of the importance of knowing the closeness of our Lord in the peaceful hours in order to be triumphant when the storms and trials of life come upon us. Let us now make our prayer the prayer of this great hymn in the assurance that the Lord's presence and power will sustain us in the hour of need.

> *I need Thee every hour, most gracious Lord.*
> *No tender voice like Thine can peace afford.*
> *I need thee every hour; stay Thou near by.*
> *Temptations lose their pow'r when Thou art nigh.*
>
> *I need Thee every hour, in joy or pain.*
> *Come quickly, and abide, or life is vain.*
> *I need Thee every hour; teach me Thy will,*
> *And Thy rich promises in me fulfill.*
>
> *I need Thee, O I need Thee;*
> *Every hour I need Thee!*
> *O bless me now, my Savior —*
> *I come to Thee.*

Let us thank God for his prevenient grace, his grace that goes before us to prepare the way for times of testing and trial. How marvelous is his grace to us.

19 Precious Lord, Take My Hand

From the Loss of a Wife in Childbirth

After he gave his life to Christ, blues entertainer "Georgia Tom" became one of the best-known leaders in gospel music of his day. Born in 1899, Thomas A. Dorsey wrote about three hundred gospel songs and directed choirs for more than fifty years, most of that time in Chicago.

The most famous song of this black gospel composer was one given by God in the night, a song of prayer born in a moment of deep sorrow. Dorsey's wife was due to bear their first child when he was called to sing at a series of revival meetings in St. Louis. He was reluctant, but his wife persuaded him to go.

During the first night of meetings a telegram was brought to him while he was on the platform. It told the tragic news that his wife had died giving birth to their son. He drove back to Chicago and within a few hours his infant son also was called home. He buried his wife and son in the same casket.

In his despondency he went to visit a friend. After walking and talking he went to a room with a piano, sat down and began to improvise on the keyboard. He found himself composing a melody and began to sing the words that God gave him "through the storm, through the night."

> *Precious Lord, take my hand,*
> *Lead me on, help me stand,*
> *I am tired, I am weak, I am worn.*
> *Through the storm, through the night,*
> *Lead me on to the light.*

Take my hand, precious Lord,
Lead me home.

When my way grows drear,
Precious Lord, linger near —
When my life is almost gone.
Hear my cry, hear my call,
Hold my hand lest I fall —
Take my hand, Precious Lord,
Lead me home.

When darkness appears,
And night draws near,
And the day is past and gone,
At the river I stand,
Guide my feet, hold my hand
Take my hand, precious Lord,
Lead me home.

Thomas Dorsey's song has sung its way in hearts around the world. It speaks a prayer that we all have need to offer. In our hurtings and in our weakness, in our storms and in our sorrows, and in the night seasons of our soul, we come to the place where we need to pray, "Precious Lord, take my hand."

How assuring to know that the Lord has promised: "For I am the Lord your God, who takes hold of your right hand and says to you, Do not fear, I will help you" (Isa. 41:13). May we know the strong and comforting hand of God, taking hold of our hand, helping and guiding us through the storms and stresses of life.

III SONGS OF SALVATION

20 Just as I Am

The World's Greatest
Soul-Winning Hymn

The hymn "Just as I Am" has been called the world's greatest soul-winning hymn, influencing more people to Christ than has any other. D. L. Moody said that this hymn drew as many people to the Lord in his fruitful evangelistic meetings as any sermons he ever preached.

As a young man, Billy Graham walked to the altar to accept Christ while "Just as I Am" was being sung. Since then, in his crusades on every continent, he has used this song as the invitation hymn, with hundreds of thousands coming to Christ as it has been sung.

Charlotte Elliott was born in England in 1789. After living a carefree life, she became a bedridden invalid by her early thirties and sank into despondency and rebellion against God. Her father invited as a guest to their home a noted minister and musician, praying that he might help mellow the soul of his talented but rebellious daughter.

Following one of her emotional outbursts at the dinner table, the minister, sensing her spiritual distress, said, "You are tired of yourself, aren't you? You are holding on to your hate and anger and have become sour, bitter and resentful." In response to this diagnosis of her heart, she unburdened herself, releasing pent-up feelings and struggles of many years.

She then asked how she could know the peace and joy of Christ. Her minister friend counseled, "You must come just as you are, a sinner, to the Lamb of God, with your fightings, fears, hates, quick temper and pride, and He will give His great love in their place." She trusted fully in

Christ and found inner peace and joy despite a physical affliction that lasted until her death at the age of eighty-two.

Each year thereafter she celebrated as her spiritual birthday that day when she was led from despair to faith in Christ. The timeless truth of that discovery had burned itself into her soul, and in 1836, fourteen years after her conversion experience, she penned her spiritual autobiography in the stanzas of this enduring hymn.

After her death, more than a thousand letters were found among her papers expressing gratitude for the help of this hymn. God used an invalid to bless the world through this song. Only eternity will reveal the countless number of souls who have found Christ through this great hymn.

> *Just as I am, without one plea,*
> > *But that thy blood was shed for me,*
> *And that thou bid'st me come to thee,*
> > *O Lamb of God, I come!*

> *Just as I am, and waiting not*
> > *To rid my soul of one dark blot,*
> *To thee whose blood can cleanse each spot,*
> > *O Lamb of God, I come!*

> *Just as I am, though tossed about*
> > *With many a conflict, many a doubt,*
> *Fightings within and fears without,*
> > *O Lamb of God, I come!*

> *Just as I am, thou wilt receive,*
> > *Wilt welcome, pardon, cleanse, relieve,*
> *Because thy promise I believe,*
> > *O Lamb of God, I come!*

> *Just as I am, thy love unknown*
> > *Has broken every barrier down,*
> *Now to be thine, yea, thine alone,*
> > *O Lamb of God, I come!*

The reason for the great success of this hymn is that it speaks one of the most fundamental spiritual truths for every life. We must come to Christ just as we are — with all of our conflicts, doubts, fears, and failures

— and he "will welcome, pardon, cleanse, relieve." May we in our heart of hearts find the peace and joy that comes when we pray, "Just as I am . . . O Lamb of God, I come."

21 In Times like These

Amid the Death and Destruction of War

Death and destruction raged throughout the world. World War II was at its height. In that ominous and dark night of our earth's history, amid the strains of wartime living, Ruth Caye Jones (1902–72) composed the song that has been a blessing and comfort in many circumstances of distress.

> *In times like these you need a Savior,*
> *In times like these you need an anchor;*
> *Be very sure, be very sure*
> *Your anchor holds and grips the Solid Rock!*
>
> *This Rock is Jesus,*
> *Yes, He's the One;*
> *This Rock is Jesus,*
> *The only One!*
> *Be very sure your anchor holds*
> *And grips the Solid Rock!*
>
> *In times like these you need the Bible,*
> *In times like these O be not idle;*
> *Be very sure, Be very sure*
> *Your anchor holds and grips the Solid Rock!*
>
> *In times likes these I have a Savior,*
> *In times like these I have an anchor;*

I'm very sure, I'm very sure
My anchor holds and grips the Solid Rock!

The Bible warns that world events will only get worse as we come to the end of this age and the return of Christ. Our children and grandchildren may well face crises unimagined in our lifetime. Amid the unsettling confusion and chaos of the world, we may affirm with another hymn writer: "On Christ the Solid Rock I stand,/All other ground is sinking sand."

The timeless message of this hymn can be appropriated for all difficult situations. An illness, a trial, a tragedy, a crisis, a death, a demanding task — all call for the stabilizing and sustaining presence of Christ in our lives. He is the only Rock to which our anchor of faith will hold steadfast amid the storms of life.

May we, in whatever circumstances come our way, with the composer of this hymn be able to say, "In times like these I have a Savior." Then the storm may rage around us, but our anchor will hold because it "grips the Solid Rock."

22 The Love of God

From the Wall of a Mental Institution

Could we with ink the ocean fill
And were the skies of parchment made,
Were ev'ry stalk on earth a quill
And ev'ry man a scribe by trade,
To write the love of God above
Would drain the ocean dry,
Nor could the scroll contain the whole
Tho stretched from sky to sky.

This magnificent verse was part of a Jewish poem found penciled on the wall of a patient's room in an insane asylum after his death. Composed in the year 1096 by Rabbi Mayer in Germany, it is believed to have been written in moments of sanity. The poem describes how the Jews had been persecuted throughout the ages for their faith. It resonates with the theme of God's eternal love and concern for his people.

Frederick Martin Lehman, a Nazarene pastor, publisher, and song writer, wrote two additional verses and set them to music to give to us one of the most eloquent hymns on the love of God.

The love of God is greater far
Than tongue or pen can ever tell,
It goes beyond the highest star
And reaches to the lowest hell;
The guilty pair, bowed down with care,

God gave His Son to win;
His erring child He reconciled
And pardoned from his sin.

When years of time shall pass away
And earthly thrones and kingdoms fall,
When men, who here refuse to pray,
On rocks and hills and mountains call,
God's love so sure shall still endure,
All measureless and strong;
Redeeming grace to Adam's race —
The saints' and angels' song.

Each Advent season we celebrate God's stupendous expression of love. The Incarnation — God becoming man — is the supreme articulation of God's love for us. "For God so loved the world that He gave His one and only Son, that whoever believes in him shall not perish but have eternal life" (John 3:16). In the words of another hymnodist: "Love so amazing, so divine,/Demands my life, my soul, my all."

23 Let the Lower Lights Be Burning

From the Story of a Shipwreck

Dwight L. Moody, famed evangelist of the last century, often told in a sermon the moving story of a ship nearing the Cleveland harbor during a violent storm on Lake Erie.

On a dark, stormy night, when the waves rolled like mountains and not a star was to be seen, a boat, rocking and plunging, neared the Cleveland harbor. "Are you sure this is Cleveland?" asked the Captain, seeing only the light from the lighthouse. "Quite sure, sir," replied the pilot.

"But where are the lower lights, the lights along the shore?" the Captain asked. "Gone out, sir!" was the reply.

"Can we make the harbor?"

"We must, or perish, sir."

With a strong hand and a brave heart, the old pilot turned the wheel. But alas, in the darkness he missed the channel and, with a crash upon the rocks, the boat was slivered and many a life lost in a watery grave.

"The Master will take care of the great lighthouse," concluded Mr. Moody. "But let us keep the lower lights burning."

Listening intently to Moody's story was Philip P. Bliss, a gospel song writer and a soloist for Moody's evangelistic meetings. Upon hearing this story Bliss was inspired to write the words and music for the well-known hymn "Let the Lower Lights Be Burning."

Brightly beams our Father's mercy
From His lighthouse evermore,
But to us He gives the keeping
Of the lights along the shore.

Let the lower lights be burning!
Send a gleam across the wave!
Some poor fainting, struggling seaman
You may rescue, you may save.

Dark the night of sin has settled,
Loud the angry billows roar;
Eager eyes are watching, longing,
For the lights along the shore.

Trim your feeble lamp, my brother!
Some poor sailor tempest tossed,
Trying now to make the harbor,
In the darkness may be lost.

Indeed, there are people who will perish without Christ unless we let our lives shine for him. Loved ones, friends, neighbors, or associates may need us as the "lower lights" to point them to the Light of the world.

You may be the only light in someone's darkness. Let us hear and heed the Master's own words: "Let your light shine before men, that they may see your good deeds and praise your Father in Heaven" (Matt. 5:16).

24 He the Pearly Gates Will Open

From a Night of Spiritual Struggle

Fredrick Arvid Blom (1867–1927), born in Sweden, came to the United States and became a Salvation Army officer in Chicago. Later he left the Army to study in a seminary and become a pastor with the Evangelical Covenant Church. Sadly, Blom backslid, and eventually went to prison. He recorded: "I drifted from God and became embittered with myself and the world."

Sometime later, at a Salvation Army meeting, Blom returned to the Lord and was able to resume a pastorate at a Swedish Congregational Church in Pennsylvania until returning to Sweden in 1921.

Shortly after his release from prison and his spiritual restoration he wrote verses that vividly describe his backslidden condition and the joy of his restored fellowship with the Lord. His words, born out of the night of his spiritual struggle and release, later wedded to music, have become a popular hymn of the Christian faith:

> *Love divine, so great and wondrous!*
> *Deep and mighty, pure, sublime!*
> *Coming from the heart of Jesus —*
> *Just the same thru tests of time.*

> *He the pearly gates will open,*
> *So that I may enter in;*
> *For He purchased my redemption*
> *And forgave me all my sin.*

> *Like a dove when hunted, frightened,*
> *Weak and helpless — so was I;*
> *Wounded, fallen, yet He healed me —*
> *He will heed the sinner's cry.*
>
> *Love divine, so great and wondrous!*
> *All my sins He then forgave!*
> *I will sing His praise forever,*
> *For His blood, his pow'r to save.*
>
> *In life's eventide, at twilight,*
> *At His door; I'll knock and wait;*
> *By the precious love of Jesus*
> *I shall enter heaven's gate.*

These words remind us that we do not need to fear death. It becomes the doorway to our eternal home with God, who will welcome us to the joys he has prepared for us. Let us then, as redeemed children of God, claim the precious promise: "No eye has seen, no ear has heard, no mind has conceived what God has prepared for those who love him" (2 Cor. 2:9).

IV SONGS OF THE CROSS

25 The Old Rugged Cross

The Most Popular Hymn

Pollsters report that "The Old Rugged Cross" is the most frequently requested hymn. Songbook editors have designated it as the most popular of all hymns. Within thirty years of its publication in 1913 more than twenty million copies had been sold, outselling every other musical composition to that date.

"The Old Rugged Cross" declares in simple and yet sublime words the central truth of the gospel, and it speaks to the need of every believer.

George Bennard, its composer, made a personal commitment to Christ while attending a Salvation Army revival meeting in Lucas, Iowa. As a young man George entered the ranks of Salvation Army officership. He initially served alone, and then with his wife, for eight years. Resigning his position with the Army, he became an evangelist in the Methodist Church.

A trying experience caused him to reflect seriously on the meaning of the cross and of Paul's writing of entering into the fellowship of Christ's suffering. We do not know what Bennard's trial was, but out of it came his conviction that the cross is not just a religious symbol but the very heart of the gospel.

Bennard later recorded, "The words of the hymn were put into my heart in answer to my own need." Out of Bennard's night of pain and prayer came the song that has blessed a worldwide fellowship of God's soldiers of the cross.

In 1958, at the age of eighty-six, George Bennard exchanged his cross for a crown.

On a hill far away
Stood an old rugged cross,
The emblem of suff'ring and shame;
And I love that old cross
Where the dearest and best
For a world of lost sinners was slain.

So I'll cherish the old rugged cross,
Till my trophies at last I lay down;
I will cling to the old rugged cross,
And exchange it some day for a crown.

O that old rugged cross,
So despised by the world,
Has a wondrous attraction for me;
For the dear Lamb of God
Left His glory above
To bear it to dark Calvary.

In that old rugged cross,
Stained with blood so divine,
A wondrous beauty I see;
For 'twas on that old cross
Jesus suffered and died
To pardon and sanctify me.

To the old rugged cross
I will ever be true,
Its shame and reproach gladly bear;
Then He'll call me some day
To my home far away,
Where His glory forever I'll share.

May we know the salvation and life eternal that comes by faith in the One who made the supreme sacrifice for us on that old rugged cross.

26 In the Cross of Christ I Glory

The Preeminence of the Cross

Portuguese settlers once built a massive cathedral on a hill overlooking the harbor of Macao, China. But a typhoon destroyed the work of human hands and the building lay in ruins except for the front wall. Towering above that high wall, surviving the elements down through the years, stands a great bronze cross.

Legend holds that when Sir John Bowring (1792–1872) saw it in 1825, he was moved to write the words of what has become one of the greatest hymns of Christendom. His four quatrains eloquently speak of the historic preeminence of the cross and its meaning in the deep and contrasting experiences of life. On Bowring's tombstone is inscribed the words, "In the cross of Christ I glory."

> *In the cross of Christ I glory,*
> *Towering o'er the wrecks of time;*
> *All the light of sacred story*
> *Gathers round its head sublime.*
>
> *When the woes of life o'ertake me,*
> *Hopes deceive and fears annoy;*
> *Never shall the cross forsake me:*
> *Lo! it glows with peace and joy.*
>
> *When the sun of bliss is beaming*
> *Light and love upon my way,*

> *From the cross the radiance streaming*
> *Adds more luster to the day.*
>
> *Bane and blessing, pain and pleasure,*
> *By the cross are sanctified;*
> *Peace is there that knows no measure,*
> *Joys that through all time abide.*

The cross remains the great symbol of our faith. It is claimed that four hundred different forms or designs of it have been in use. The cross reminds us of the infinite price paid for our salvation. The apostle Paul, exalting in its meaning, said, "May I never boast except in the cross of our Lord Jesus Christ" (Gal. 6:14). May our glory, our boasting, be alone in the cross of our Lord, the cross that became the supreme proclamation of God's love for each of us.

27 Beneath the Cross of Jesus

From One Who Followed the Way of the Cross

The cross is the sacred symbol of the Christian faith. There our burden of sin was lifted. There we experienced the wonderful grace of our Lord and Savior. Our sins and guilt were all nailed to that cross. Since we came to that old rugged cross, life has never been the same. There we found salvation and life abundant and eternal.

One of the great hymns of the cross was written by Elizabeth Clephane (1830–69) of Scotland. She learned the meaning of the cross when as a young child she lost both her parents. From her youth she was in delicate health. Although frail, she gave herself in service to the poor and sick.

She took seriously the challenge of the cross when Christ said, "Whoever will come after me, let him deny himself and take up his cross and follow me" (Matt. 16:24). Along with her sister, she gave all of her earthly goods, except dire necessities, to charity, including their horse and carriage. Her acts of compassion among the sick and suffering earned from the townspeople the affectionate designation, "The Sunbeam."

One of her two enduring hymns, "There Were Ninety and Nine," was made famous by Ira Sankey during Moody's revivals in the United States and Great Britain.

Shortly before her death at the early age of thirty-nine, from serious illness and weakness, she composed "Beneath the Cross of Jesus." The Scots knew their Bible. Her imagery is biblical: "the mighty rock" (Isa. 32:2), "weary land" (Ps. 63:1), "home within the wilderness" (Jer. 9:2), "rest upon the way" (Isa. 28:12), "noontide heat" (Isa. 4:6), "burden of the day" (Matt. 11:30).

In the second verse the cross becomes more than a symbol. On it the lyricist sees "the very form of One dying there for me." She sees two contrasting wonders — the wonder of God's love and the wonder of our unworthiness (editors have softened her original "worthlessness").

> Beneath the cross of Jesus
>   I fain would take my stand,
> The shadow of a mighty rock
>   Within a weary land;
> A home within the wilderness,
>   A rest upon the way,
> From the burning of the noontide heat
>   And the burden of the day.
>
> Upon that cross of Jesus
>   Mine eye at times can see
> The very dying form of One
>   Who suffered there for me;
> And from my smitten heart, with tears,
>   Two wonders I confess:
> The wonders of His glorious love,
>   And my own worthlessness.
>
> I take, O Cross, thy shadow
>   For my abiding place;
> I ask no other sunshine than
>   The sunshine of His face;
> Content to let the world go by,
>   To know no gain nor loss,
> My sinful self my only shame,
>   My glory all the Cross.

Miss Clephane did not live to hear either of her two hymns put to music or to know the great blessing that they brought to an innumerable company throughout the world. The words of this frail Scot saint speak eloquently of what the cross should mean to us. May this inspiring hymn be our experience and testimony, that our glory will be "all the cross."

28 When I Survey the Wondrous Cross

Contemplating the Meaning of Calvary

He was only five feet tall, with a large head made bigger by a huge wig, and with a hooked nose and a frail and sickly body. Such was the appearance of the illustrious Dr. Isaac Watts (1674–1748). As a young man he had proposed to a lovely lady. In refusing she said, "I like the jewel but not the setting."

Illnesses plagued him throughout his life, and for most of his last thirty years he was an invalid. But his brilliant mind refused to be subdued by his frail body, and he wrote a prodigious number of books and more than six hundred hymns, including such enduring ones as "Jesus Shall Reign," "O God Our Help in Ages Past," and the Christmas carol "Joy to the World."

Dr. Watts's songs helped prepare the way for the great revivals under the Wesleys and Whitefield. He is memorialized in Westminster Abbey with a tablet picturing him writing at a table while angels whisper songs in his ear.

Watts was driven to write religious verse by the lamentable singing in the churches of his day. He said, "The singing of God's praise is the part of worship nighest heaven, and its performance among us is the worst on earth." One Sunday after returning from a morning worship he considered to be dreadful, he complained to his father that the hymns sung at that time were so tuneless. His father smiled and suggested that he provide something better.

During that afternoon he wrote his first hymn. In the evening service the hymn was lined out and sung, and thus began the revolution of English hymn singing. He went on to create the model for English hymns and became known as "the Father of English Hymnody." His *Hymns and Spiritual Songs,* published in 1707, became the first hymnbook in the English language.

Watts reached the high point of his devotional poetry with his classic, "When I Survey the Wondrous Cross." His words speak of our response to the matchless sacrifice of Christ on the cross. We confess our poverty of language when dealing with this sublime theme that deserves the eloquence of angels. But Isaac Watts comes as close as human expression can to a worthy response to Calvary.

The words of this hymn were inspired by the apostle Paul's impassioned declaration of Galatians 6:14: "May I never boast except in the cross of our Lord Jesus Christ."

In the opening line, "survey" suggests not mere sight but contemplation on the meaning of Calvary. The cross is "wondrous" because this instrument of death became God's means for redeeming a world. "Prince of Glory" speaks of the highest exaltation of the Savior. In the light of the cross we are led to "pour contempt" on our pride.

In the final couplet of the third stanza Watts loses himself in adoration until even the crown of thorns becomes more priceless than a king's diadem. The hymn climaxes with a realization and surrender to this amazing love that "demands my soul, my life, my all."

> *When I survey the wondrous cross*
> *On which the Prince of Glory died,*
> *My richest gain I count but loss,*
> *And pour contempt on all my pride.*
>
> *Forbid it Lord, that I should boast*
> *Save in the death of Christ, my God;*
> *All the vain things that charm me most,*
> *I sacrifice them to his blood.*
>
> *See, from his head, his hands, his feet,*
> *Sorrow and love flow mingled down;*
> *Did e'er such love and sorrow meet,*
> *Or thorns compose so rich a crown?*

Were the whole realm of nature mine,
That were a present far too small;
Love so amazing, so divine,
Demands my soul, my life, my all.

During each Lenten season we again contemplate the message and meaning of Calvary. May the imagery, insight, and passion of this enduring hymn lead us to deeper devotion to the Son of God, who on a felon's cross paid the supreme price for our salvation.

29 Am I a Soldier of the Cross?

A Painful Memory

Isaac Watts had painful memories of his early years. His parents were Dissenters, people whose religious affiliation was outside of the Church of England, the state church. Dissenters often suffered persecution in the seventeenth century.

His father, a deacon in the Congregational Church, was arrested and imprisoned several times. When Isaac was an infant, his mother would sit on a stone opposite the jail and nurse her baby while visiting her husband. Fifteen years later, the Toleration Act of 1689 granted freedom of worship for Dissenters. Isaac was old enough then to remember the persecution when religious freedom was denied.

When he was twenty-five years old, he became assistant pastor of the Mark Lane Independent Chapel, London, and three years later became its pastor. Often he would write a hymn for the congregation to sing at the conclusion of the Sunday service. Remembering the suffering for the faith and the courage of his father, he one Sunday preached on "Holy Fortitude," using the text: "Stand firm in the faith; be men of courage; be strong" (1 Cor. 16:13). The preacher/poet wrote to be sung following that sermon a hymn that challenges all of us to be "soldiers of the cross."

> *Am I a soldier of the cross,*
> *A follower of the Lamb,*
> *And shall I fear to own his cause,*
> *Or blush to speak His name?*

> *Must I be carried to the skies*
> *On flow'ry beds of ease,*
> *While others fought to win the prize*
> *And sailed thru stormy seas?*
>
> *Are there no foes for me to face?*
> *Must I not stem the flood?*
> *Is this vile world a friend to grace,*
> *To help me on to God?*
>
> *Sure I must fight if I would reign.*
> *Increase my courage, Lord.*
> *I'll bear the toil, endure the pain,*
> *Supported by thy Word.*

Life often becomes filled with painful memories. But, as with Isaac Watts, when our remembrances are surrendered to the Lord, he turns them into songs of courage and faith.

"Jesus has many lovers of His heavenly kingdom, but few bearers of His cross," wrote Thomas à Kempis. The cost of discipleship has never been lowered. There are no bargain rates. As of old, Jesus still calls to would-be disciples: "If anyone would come after me, he must deny himself and take up his cross and follow me" (Matt. 16:24).

Isaac Watts witnessed in the persecution of his parents what it meant to be a "soldier of the cross." His hymn echoes Christ's challenge of the cross, calling us not to a frolic but to a fight, not to a picnic but to a pilgrimage, not to self-indulgence but to self-denial, and not to comfort but to the cross.

30 He Never Said a Mumblin' Word

Pain Set to Music

America's embrace of slavery was the darkest chapter in its history. But amid this monstrous evil with its horror of oppression and dehumanization, God kept his promise. He gave to his people a song in the night. In fact, to the African Diaspora, he gave a whole symphony of songs — the Negro Spirituals — that have immeasurably enriched our musical heritage.

Someone has said the Negro Spirituals are "pain set to music." Eloquent witness of this truth are the words, "Nobody knows the trouble I've seen. Nobody knows, but Jesus . . . Glory Hallelujah!" It begins with pain and ends with praise. It starts with trouble and ends with triumph. People who can begin and end a song like this have something to give to the world.

W. E. B. DuBois in *The Souls of Black Folk* says that these compositions are "the music of an unhappy people, of the children of disappointment." He adds that their songs "tell of death and suffering and unvoiced longing toward a truer world."

Martin Luther King Jr., at the forefront of innumerable freedom marches and mass meetings, said, "An important part of the mass meeting was the freedom songs. In a sense the freedom songs are the soul of the movement."

The spirituals have been a special genre of sacred music, poignant and powerful expressions of protest and praise. The history of the Afro-American odyssey from slavery to freedom is seen through the prism of its music.

72

This repertoire has included such traditional songs as "Swing Low, Sweet Chariot," "Standing in the Need of Prayer," "Were You There When They Crucified My Lord?," "Steal Away to Jesus," "Let Us Break Bread Together on Our Knees," "We Are Climbing Jacob's Ladder."

One of my own most moving musical experiences was to hear Marian Anderson sing "He Never Said a Mumblin' Word." Toscanini said that Miss Anderson had "a voice that is given but once in a century." Her peerless contralto voice in that moving spiritual portrayed with eloquent pathos the suffering of our Lord as no other song I have ever heard. Only a race that had suffered could write such a song. Her audience was transfixed in those moments as she moved through the verses of that soul-stirring spiritual.

> *See how they done my Lord,*
> *And He never said a mumblin' word,*
> *See how they done my lord,*
> *And He never said a mumblin' word,*
> *See how they done my Lord,*
> *And He never said a mumblin' word —*
> *My Lord, He never said a mumblin' word.*
>
> *They led Him into Pilate's hall,*
> *And He never said a mumblin' word,*
> *They led Him into Pilate's hall,*
> *And He never said a mumblin' word.*
> *They led Him into Pilate's hall,*
> *And He never said a mumblin' word —*
> *My Lord, He never said a mumblin' word.*
>
> *They put on Him a thorny crown,*
> *And He never said a mumblin' word,*
> *They put on Him a thorny crown,*
> *And He never said a mumblin' word.*
> *They put on Him a thorny crown,*
> *And He never said a mumblin' word —*
> *My Lord, He never said a mumblin' word.*
>
> *They put on Him a purple robe,*
> *And He never said a mumblin' word,*
> *They put on Him a purple robe,*

And He never said a mumblin' word.
They put on Him a purple robe,
And He never said a mumblin' word —
My Lord, he never said a mumblin' word.

They nailed Him to the cross,
And He never said a mumblin' word,
They nailed Him to the cross,
And He never said a mumblin' word.
They nailed Him to the cross,
And He never said a mumblin' word —
My Lord, He never said a mumblin' word.

He suffered on the cross,
And He never said a mumblin' word,
He suffered on the cross,
And He never said a mumblin' word.
He suffered on the cross,
And He never said a mumblin' word —
My Lord, He never said a mumblin' word.

They pierced Him in the side,
And He never said a mumblin' word,
They pierced Him in the side,
And He never said a mumblin' word.
They pierced Him in the side,
And He never said a mumblin' word —
My Lord, He never said a mumblin' word.

He bowed His head and died,
And He never said a mumblin' word,
He bowed His head and died,
And He never said a mumblin' word.
He bowed His head and died,
And He never said a mumblin' word —
My Lord, He never said a mumblin' word.

The cross of Calvary has resonated in songs of devotion, such as this moving spiritual, that speak to the depth of our hearts.

31 Were You There When They Crucified My Lord?

From the Cauldron of Slavery

We are all heavy debtors to Afro-Americans of the southland in pre–Civil War days for some of the most beautiful, touching, and inspiring songs our nation knows — Negro Spirituals. Someone has beautifully termed them "Songs of the Spirit."

These great songs were first played upon heartstrings taut with the oppression of slavery. The unnamed black bards have given to us one of our richest treasures of devotional music from the antebellum days when religion and songs were their consolation.

The children of Africa, for example, readily adopted the Hebrew exodus story as their own with such songs as:

> When Israel was in Egypt's land
> Let my people go,
> Oppressed so hard they could not stand,
> Let my people go.

The crucifixion of Jesus struck a responsive chord in the heart of the slaves. They identified with the sufferings of their Lord, who had felt the sting of the lash, the injustice and oppression of inhuman treatment. With their taskmasters whipping them into submission, lynching their men, raping their women, and selling their children, the slave could identify with the One crucified on a felon's cross. The slaves would sing with intense pathos, "Nobody knows the trouble I've seen."

The tragedy of Calvary is dramatically portrayed in "Were You There When They Crucified My Lord?" The unknown composer goes beyond the horror of Calvary to the triumph of our Lord over the cross and death. His question-and-answer format makes the words all the more poignantly personal.

Were you there when they crucified my Lord?
Were you there when they crucified my Lord?
Oh! sometimes it causes me to tremble, tremble, tremble,
Were you there when they crucified my Lord?

Were you there when they pierced Him in the side?
Were you there when they pierced Him in the side?
Oh! sometimes it causes me to tremble, tremble, tremble.
Were you there when they pierced Him in the side?

Were you there when the sun refused to shine?
Were you there when the sun refused to shine?
Oh! sometimes it causes me to tremble, tremble, tremble,
Were you there when the sun refused to shine?

Were you there when they laid Him in the tomb?
Were you there when they laid Him in the tomb?
Oh! sometimes it causes me to tremble, tremble, tremble,
Were you there when they laid Him in the tomb?

Were you there when He rose from the dead?
Were you there when He rose from the dead?
Oh! sometimes it causes me to tremble, tremble, tremble.
Were you there when He rose from the dead?

Were you there when He ascended on high?
Were you there when He ascended on high?
Oh! sometimes it causes me to tremble, tremble, tremble,
Were you there when He ascended on high?

The unnamed composers of these poignant and powerful spirituals had a faith that saw God's ultimate triumph beyond earth's tragedies and injustice. God will also give us a song in our night season that will enable us to see beyond the cross to the crown, beyond Good Friday to Easter Sunday and Ascension Day.

Let us hear the accents of God's love and triumph in the song that he gives to us in our night season.

32 Into the Woods
My Master Went

Renewal in the Mountain

Sidney Lanier (1841–81), southern poet, in his brief life of thirty-nine years, had a remarkable record of fourteen volumes of prose and ten books of poetry. Yet he struggled all of his life against poverty, disease, and disappointment.

Lanier served in the Confederate Army during the Civil War, was captured, and held prisoner until the end of the war. The hardships of imprisonment were to take a heavy toll on his health.

After the war he became the outstanding flutist in the country, playing with the Peabody Orchestra in Baltimore. He also lectured on English Literature at Johns Hopkins University. Weakened by the ravages of tuberculosis, his health gave way and he had to retreat to the mountains of North Carolina.

There he meditated on the final hours of Jesus, also doomed to die before his time. He thought on how our Lord retreated to the Mount of Olives for renewal and strength. His own life drawing to a close, Lanier went into the woods to find fortitude and inner peace.

No longer able to play his prized flute, no longer applauded by appreciative audiences in concert halls, his life ebbing from him, he penned "The Ballad of the Trees and the Master." These sixteen lines were destined to live among great Christian poetry and hymns. Written during his own dark night of the soul, they express the comfort and inspiration that can come from trees and the healing effect of nature on the human spirit.

"The thorn-tree had a mind to Him," speaks in powerful poetic imagery of the tree's yearning for forgiveness, for it knew that on the morrow it would form Christ's mocking crown. The hymn is appropriately sung on Good Friday eve.

> *Into the woods my Master went,*
> *Clean forspent, forspent.*
> *Into the woods my Master came,*
> *Forspent with love and shame.*
> *But the olives they were not blind to him,*
> *The thorn-tree had a mind to him*
> *When into the woods he came.*
>
> *Out of the woods my Master went,*
> *And he was well content.*
> *Out of the woods my Master came,*
> *Content with death and shame.*
> *When Death and Shame would woo him last,*
> *From under the trees they drew him last:*
> *'Twas on a tree they slew him — last*
> *When out of the woods he came.*

V SONGS OF DEVOTION

33 O Love That Will Not Let Me Go

A Classic Forged out of Blindness

Out of the crucible of his own suffering, George Matheson gave us the devotional treasure "O Love That Will Not Let Me Go."

Born in Scotland in 1842, from his earliest childhood Matheson was troubled with failing sight. By the time he was eighteen his loss was total. In spite of this handicap he distinguished himself as a brilliant student at Edinburgh University, earning a doctorate. Later he established himself as an eminent preacher and writer and was honored by an invitation from Queen Victoria to preach at Balmoral Castle.

When the young lady to whom he was engaged found that he had become totally blind, she refused to marry him. Out of that rejection he wrote of a love that was steadfast and unfailing amid all the circumstances of life.

> O love, that wilt not let me go,
>   I rest my weary soul in Thee;
> I give Thee back the life I owe,
> That in Thine ocean depths its flow
>   May richer, fuller be.

And out of his blindness and physical darkness, he affirmed:

> O Light, that followest all my way
>   I yield my flickering torch to Thee;

> *My heart restores its borrowed ray,*
> *That in Thy sunshine's blaze its day*
> *May brighter, fairer be.*

Dr. Matheson's hymn employs great metaphors to express his inspired insights. The first and second symbols in this hymn are love and light. The symbol of his third verse is joy. It is a joy that overtakes pain, with the rainbow emerging out of the storm, the tearless morning succeeding the tearful night. Although for him beauty was eclipsed, he lyricized:

> *O joy that seekest me through pain,*
> *I cannot close my heart to thee;*
> *I trace the rainbow through the rain*
> *And feel the promise is not vain,*
> *That morn shall tearless be.*

The hymn climaxes with the great metaphor of the cross. From the crucifixion of Christ and of self comes life eternal:

> *O cross that liftest up my head,*
> *I dare not ask to fly from thee;*
> *I lay in dust life's glory dead,*
> *And from the ground there blossoms red*
> *Life that shall endless be.*

Dr. Matheson has given his own record of the composing of this song: "Something had happened that caused me the most severe mental suffering. The hymn was the fruit of that suffering. It was the quickest bit of work I ever did in my life. I had the impression of having it dictated to me by some inward voice rather than my having worked it out myself. The whole work was completed in five minutes, and it never received at my hands any alterations or corrections."

How wonderful that from so unlovely a thing as suffering can come so exquisite an offering as this poem. Its lofty language and depth of devotional expression gives it a place among the classic hymns of our faith. It stands in stark contrast to the saccharine and shallow expressions that can sometimes characterize modern singing.

May the love, light, joy, and cross of which it speaks be our experience in Christ.

34 Take My Life and Let It Be

A Prayer Lived Out in Life

Frances Ridley Havergal (1836–79) of England began writing verse at age seven. Her insatiable thirst for the Bible led her to memorize the entire New Testament, Psalms, Isaiah, and the Minor Prophets. She was a concert contralto soloist and a brilliant classical pianist. She gave her life to Christ at age fifteen.

At age twenty-one she stood in the art gallery at Dusseldorf, Germany, looking at the painting of the crucifixion with the engraving beneath it: "This I have done for thee; what hast thou done for Me?" In the previous century the wealthy young Count Zinzendorf of Moravian missionary fame read these same words and was led to consecrate his life to Christ. As she stood there, her very soul was stirred. Tears cascaded down her cheeks. From that moment she dedicated her talents to the service of the Lord.

Throughout her life she was frail and delicate in health and died at the early age of forty-two. When she wrote "Take my life, and let it be consecrated, Lord, to Thee," it was for her a prayer. And when she penned the words, "Take my silver and my gold," she did exactly that! She gave fifty pieces of jewelry (heirlooms) to the Church Missionary Society, including a jewel cabinet that she said was "fit for a countess." She retained only a brooch for daily wear that was a memorial of her parents, and a locket with a portrait of her niece who had gone to heaven. Of that experience she wrote, "I don't think I need tell you I never packed a box with such pleasure."

Despite the dark nights of frequent sickness and suffering, the dedicated life of this poetess can best be summed up in her own prayer lyrics.

Take my life, and let it be
  Consecrated, Lord, to thee;
Take my moments and my days;
  Let them flow in ceaseless praise.

Take my hands, and let them move
  At the impulse of thy love;
Take my feet, and let them be
  Swift and beautiful for thee.

Take my voice, and let me sing
  Always, only for my King;
Take my lips, and let them be
  Filled with messages from thee.

Take my silver and my gold,
  Not a mite would I withhold;
Take my intellect, and use
  Every power as thou shalt choose.

Take my will, and make it thine,
  It shall be no longer mine;
Take my heart, it is thine own,
  It shall be thy royal throne.

Take my love, my Lord, I pour
  At thy feet its treasure-store;
Take myself, and I will be
  Ever, only, all for thee.

  May the words of this beautiful hymn echo the prayer and consecration of our life.

35 Jesus, the Very Thought of Thee

A Light from the Dark Ages

Bernard of Clairvaux (1090–1153) is considered the greatest of medieval saints. Martin Luther, himself a monk, wrote of him, "He was the best monk that ever lived, whom I admire beyond all the rest put together." Born into a noble family in France, he turned his back on wealth and nobility to live as a monk and to advance the life of holiness, discipline, prayer, and ministering to the physical and spiritual needs of the people.

He and his followers hewed a home out of a wilderness of forests, a desolate haunt of robbers. The order he founded became the chief religious power in western Europe for three hundred years. Bernard's writings and poetry became his lasting legacy to the church. His fruitful contemplation of eighty-six sermons on the first two chapters of the Song of Songs is a classic of biblical exposition.

But the labors and legacy of Bernard of Clairvaux were all done in a dark and difficult time. The Middle Ages, scornfully termed "The Dark Ages," was a period of moral darkness and a corrupt church. The world of Bernard gave no encouragement for the Christian faith.

Visualize Bernard the monk, before dawn at prayer in his bare cell. Soon another day in the monotonous succession would be upon him — hard labor in the field, the constant danger of robbers, and the wickedness of men with whom he would have to deal. But now he kneels in contemplation, and his soul is filled with a sweetness that transcends the dark and difficult time in which he lived. His gifted mind gives expression to the rapture of his soul:

> Jesus, the very thought of Thee
>> With sweetness fills my breast;
> But sweeter far thy face to see,
>> And in thy presence rest.
>
> Nor voice can sing, nor heart can frame,
>> Nor can the memory find
> A sweeter sound than thy blest name,
>> O Savior of mankind.
>
> O hope of every contrite heart!
>> O joy of all the meek!
> To those who fall, how kind thou art,
>> How good to those who seek!
>
> But what to those who find? Ah! this
>> Nor tongue nor pen can show;
> The love of Jesus, what it is
>> None but his loved ones know.
>
> Jesus, our only joy be thou,
>> As thou our prize wilt be;
> Jesus, be thou our glory now
>> And through eternity.

We do not live in the Dark Ages but in an age of enlightenment. However, amid the confusion and chaos of our world, we too need to contemplate the holiness, love, and beauty of Jesus — to fill our life with the sweetness and joy of his presence.

Centuries ago a wise man wrote, "For as he thinks in his heart, so is he" (Prov. 23:7). Let us meditate and think more upon Christ and then more of his likeness shall be seen in us.

36 Strong Son of God

The Death of a Friend

Alfred Tennyson left giant prints upon the sands of literature as he strode through the exciting Victorian era. The reader of his memorable lines finds spiritual convictions as strong undercurrents in the forceful tides of his thought. He once said, "It is hard to believe in God; but it is harder not to believe in God. My most passionate desire is to have a clearer vision of God."

His Christian faith is perhaps best expressed in two poems: "In Memoriam" and "Crossing the Bar." The latter was directed by the poet to be the final poem in any published anthology of his work. It is often quoted at funeral services, with its affirmation: "I hope to see my Pilot face to face when I have crossed the bar."

The early and shocking death of his college classmate and very close friend, Arthur Hallam, was a traumatic experience. Hallam almost becomes ubiquitous in Tennyson's writings. The poet's constant sorrow led him to become a diarist. "In Memoriam" is a compilation of his lyrics of sorrow over the years following Hallam's death.

From the nadir of his despair and doubt the poet reaches out for ultimate answers about life and death and the individual's role in the universe. His desire for faith seems mocked by nature, which is "red in tooth and claw." However, the discerning reader perceives that doubt is not really antithetical to faith, as the poet states: "There lives more faith in honest doubt,/Believe me, than in half the creeds." The poet finds himself led to a "faith beyond the forms of faith." For God and true religion are always bigger than the molds that humans would make for them. Structures tend to impose limits. God is infinite. Tennyson was reaching beyond the finite.

His sublime Prologue to "In Memoriam" was written as a last part of that poem. But it was finally placed at the beginning as an affirmation of faith. The journey and quest of the soul as described in the poem had led to faith.

Various hymnals usually select four to seven of the original eleven stanzas. The hymn expresses Tennyson's reaction to the science and philosophy that was fast making agnostics of professing Christians. Stanza one is a prayer to immortal Love, Tennyson's name for God, as suggested in 1 John 4:8. The second couplet concludes that God's existence cannot be proved in human terms but that we can lay hold of him by faith. We believe where we cannot prove. In stanza three the poet asserts that the Son of God exemplifies the highest and holiest manhood. May these words, forged out of deep personal loss, also be our statement of faith in the "Strong Son of God."

> Strong Son of God, immortal Love,
>   Whom we, that have not seen Thy face,
> By faith, and faith alone, embrace,
> Believing where we cannot prove. . . .
>
> Thou wilt not leave us in the dust:
>   Thou madest man, he knows not why,
>   He thinks he was not made to die;
> And Thou has made him; Thou art just.
>
> Thou seemest human and divine,
>   The highest, holiest manhood, Thou.
>   Our wills are ours, we know not how;
> Our wills are ours, to make them Thine.
>
> Our little systems have their day;
>   They have their day and cease to be;
>   They are but broken lights of Thee,
> And Thou, O Lord, are more than they.

37 Near to the Heart of God

A Comfort in Grief

Job, the great sufferer, gave us his famous epigram, "Man is born to trouble as surely as sparks fly up" (Job 5:7). Trouble surely comes into each life. When it does we need a strength greater than our own to carry us through.

While serving as a pastor in Chicago in 1901, Cleland McAfee was stunned to receive within the space of twenty-four hours the shocking news that his two beloved nieces had both died from diphtheria. Crushed with grief, he turned to God and the Scriptures for comfort. He found that there is a place of comfort, of shelter, of peace in times of deep loss and grief. It is near to the heart of God.

He was led to compose a song for the comfort of his own soul as well as for his family. From his grieving heart flowed the words and tune of "Near to the Heart of God." On the day of the double funeral he stood with his choir outside of the quarantined home of his brother, singing the song that God had given to him in his night season. The following Sunday, the choir of McAfee's church sang the hymn. Soon it spread across the nation.

> *There is a place of quiet rest,*
> *Near to the heart of God,*
> *A place where sin cannot molest,*
> *Near to the heart of God.*
>
> *There is a place of comfort sweet,*
> *Near to the heart of God,*

> *A place where we our Savior meet,*
> *Near to the heart of God.*
>
> *There is a place of full release,*
> *Near to the heart of God,*
> *A place where all is joy and peace,*
> *Near to the heart of God.*
>
> *O Jesus, blest Redeemer,*
> *Sent from the heart of God,*
> *Hold us who wait before Thee*
> *Near to the heart of God.*

The assurance and prayer of this hymn can be ours in all of life's times and testings. May it be so.

38 More Love to Thee

In the Loss of Children

Elizabeth Prentiss (1818–78) had grown up in a Christian home in Portland, Maine, where her father was a respected minister. After a period teaching school she married Dr. George Prentiss, a Presbyterian minister who later became a seminary professor.

Throughout most of her life she scarcely knew what it was to be without pain. She suffered from migraine headaches and chronic insomnia. Though a lifelong invalid, she wrote and had published her poetry and prose, including the best seller at the time, *Stepping Heavenward*. The one poem that has survived in common use is her song "More Love to Thee."

It was written in 1856 during a time of great personal sorrow when the Prentisses lost their oldest child. Then tragedy struck another blow — their other child died. Elizabeth was disconsolate and devastated. In her anguish she cried out, "Our lives are wrecked, our hopes shattered, our dreams dissolved. Sometimes I don't think I can stand living for another moment, much less a lifetime."

Later she retired to the solitude of her room. Turning to her Bible and hymnal, and taking her sorrow to God in prayer, the words came to her, "More love to Thee, O Christ, more love to Thee." Her poem was not shown to anyone, not even to her husband, until thirteen years later.

Set to music by William Doane during the spiritual awakening of the early 1870s, the hymn became widely used and has appeared in church hymnals now for more than a century.

More love to Thee, O Christ,
More love to Thee!
Hear Thou the prayer I make
On bended knee;
This is my earnest plea;
More love, O Christ, to Thee,
More love to Thee,
More love to Thee!

Once earthly joy I craved,
Sought peace and rest;
Now thee alone; I seek,
Give what is best;
This all my prayer shall be:
More love, O Christ to Thee,
More love to Thee,
More love to Thee!

When we experience sorrow or tragedy, may we also learn to draw nearer to our Lord. In our expression of greater love to him, we too will find comfort and strength to go on.

39 Thou Art Enough for Me

Written from a Sickbed

William Elwin Oliphant (1860–1941) had been ordained in the Church of England and served as a curate for two years. He was attracted to The Salvation Army in 1884 and joined its ranks as an officer.

He had a distinguished career, serving in positions of divisional leadership, then as private secretary to the Chief of the Staff and later as Territorial Commander of five European countries. He wrote two books and has contributed to The Salvation Army Song Book one of its beautiful devotional hymns, "Thou Art Enough for Me."

The song was born out of a serious illness that laid him aside from his cherished ministry. William Booth, founder of The Salvation Army, was conducting an all-night prayer meeting in London in 1887, which Major Oliphant had to miss due to his illness. From his bedside he wrote the words that have brought comfort and assurance to many who, going through trial, have found Christ to be their sufficiency.

The beautiful music wed to the verses was composed by the "father of Salvation Army music," Richard Slater, following weeks of meditating upon the devotional message of the verses.

> *I kneel beside thy sacred cross,*
> *   And count for thee my life as dross;*
> *O satisfy my soul this hour*
> *   With thy dear love, my healing power.*

Thou art enough for me,
Thou art enough for me;
O precious, living, loving Lord,
Yes, thou art enough for me!

My helpless soul, rest thou in God
And lean upon his faithful word,
So in my heart, Lord, thou shalt find
That I am to thy will resigned.

Through every fear my soul doth climb
Above the things of passing time,
And to my eyes the sight is given
Which makes my earth a present Heaven.

Are you going through a time of deep need? Of seeming helplessness? Of fear for the future? Then look up to the One who said, "My grace is sufficient for thee." He will give strength and sustenance for each day and each need. From the depths of your heart, pray and affirm, "Thou art enough for me."

40 Angels, from the Realms of Glory

A Song of Worship out of Suffering

James Montgomery (1771–1854) struggled with depression throughout his life due to a great personal loss in his early years. At the age of twelve, his parents went as Moravian missionaries to the West Indies, leaving him at a seminary school in the United States. He never saw them again, as both parents died while bringing the gospel to poverty-stricken people.

Editor of a newspaper, and inspired by his parents' dedication to the people of the West Indies, he championed the cause against slavery. The controversial issues that appeared in his paper landed him in prison twice.

During one Advent season, he was lifted from his depression while contemplating the marvel of the Incarnation. He was led to pen the words of our familiar Christmas carol, "Angels, from the Realms of Glory."

This pictorial hymn first addresses the herald angels, telling them not to stay in Bethlehem but to spread the good news to all of the world. The shepherds are next invited to worship the Babe who is "God with man . . . now residing," fulfilling the glowing meaning of his name, Immanuel — "God with us."

Born in the heart and soul of one who knew the experience of lifelong suffering, these words again each Advent season resonate in celebration of the Lord who descended from glory to live among us and to become our Savior.

Angels, from the realms of Glory,
Wing your flight o'er all the earth:
Ye, who sang creation's story,
Now proclaim Messiah's birth.
    Come and worship,
Worship Christ, the new-born King.

Shepherds in the field abiding,
Watching o'er your flocks by night,
God with man is now residing;
Yonder shines the infant light.
    Come and worship,
Worship Christ, the new-born King.

Saints before the altar bending,
Watching long in hope and fear,
Suddenly the lord descending,
In his temple shall appear,
    Come and worship,
Worship Christ the new-born King.

Sinners moved by true repentance,
Doomed for guilt to endless pains,
Justice now revokes the sentence,
Mercy calls you, break your chains.
    Come and worship,
Worship Christ, the new-born King.

Let us heed the invitation that concludes each stanza of this carol: "Worship Christ, the new-born King." For that is what Christmas and the coming of Christ is truly all about.

41 Silent Night

From a Broken Organ

A crisis threatened the plans for the Christmas Eve service in 1818 in the Church of St. Nicholas in the little town of Oberndorf, Austria. The church organ was broken and could not be used for the traditional Midnight Mass.

Josef Mohr attended a nativity play in the village on the evening of December twenty-third. The young priest, inspired by the pageant, stopped on his way home at a favorite viewpoint overlooking the town. His heart was moved by the beauty of the night and the inspiration of the Christmas story. Returning home, he lit his lamp and, in its soft glow, wrote the words of *Stille Nacht.*

The next morning he took his three stanzas to the home of his friend, Franz Gruber the church organist, and said, "See if you can wed these words to a melody." Because there was no hope of the organ being repaired in time for the Midnight Mass that Christmas Eve, Gruber wrote the music for guitar. Mohr and Gruber sang their hymn that Christmas Eve to the accompaniment of Gruber's guitar and a choir of young girls from the village who repeated the last two lines in four-part harmony. Little could the simple worshipers imagine the miracle of song taking place as its pristine and pure notes flowed through the church that night. It was reminiscent of a birth, centuries before, that also took place in the humblest of villages, ultimately to have an impact upon the whole world.

Mohr and Gruber never intended for their carol to be used outside of their little mountain village. But when the organ repairman returned to complete his repairs, he heard the song. Enchanted by both verse and melody, he obtained a copy, and through his influence it spread and soon was included in concerts throughout Austria and Germany, billed as a Tyrolean folk song.

In 1839 "Silent Night, Holy Night" was first performed in the United States by a visiting group of Austrian singers. Soon it made its way into hearts around the world, becoming the best-loved Christmas carol of all time.

Silent night, holy night,
All is calm, all is bright.
Round yon virgin mother and child.
Holy infant so tender and mild,
Sleep in heavenly peace,
Sleep in heavenly peace.

Silent night, holy night,
Shepherds quake at the sight.
Glories stream from heaven afar,
Heavenly hosts sing alleluia;
Christ, the Savior, is born!
Christ, the Savior, is born!

Silent night, holy night.
Son of God, love's pure light
Radiant beams from Thy holy face,
With the dawn of redeeming grace,
Jesus, Lord, at Thy birth,
Jesus, Lord, at Thy birth.

The beauty and simplicity of this carol captures something of the wonder and majesty of Christmas. The manger is the marvel of the ages. The Babe of Bethlehem was God becoming visible to human sight, vocal to human hearing, tangible to human touch. Jesus was the heart of God wrapped in human flesh.

The Incarnation is the central fact and miracle of Christianity. Upon it depends the whole superstructure of our faith. No tongue of human nor brain of scholar can explain this mighty transition that wrapped deity in the dust and decay of human flesh. This beautiful carol reminds us each Advent season of the "dawn of redeeming grace" that broke upon the world in majestic and matchless splendor.

If the church organ had not broken down, the loveliest Christmas carol of them all might never have been known. It is often out of the brokenness of our lives that God reveals his choicest beauty and blessing. He makes of our tears a rainbow, of our thorns a crown, and of our dark nights a path upon which his love shines with an uncommon radiance.

VI SONGS OF TESTIMONY

42 Amazing Grace

From Slave Ship Owner to Salvation

One of the most popular and beloved of all hymns, "Amazing Grace," was penned by John Newton of England in the 1700s. The hymn relates the pilgrimage of its author, who was radically transformed by the grace of God.

John Newton's devout mother dedicated him early to the ministry and began his religious training at an early age. He could recite the catechism and hymns by the age of four. His mother died when he was seven, and at the age of eleven, after several years of school away from home, he went to sea with his sea captain father. Later he served in the British Navy, deserted, and when caught was put in irons and whipped in public.

Then Newton abandoned the religious principles taught by his mother and embarked on a life of such debauchery that his friends despaired of his sanity. He signed on a slave ship and soon was master of his own ship, dealing in the monstrous evil of bringing slaves from Africa. With a whip in one hand and a gun in the other, often given to drunkenness and lust, he sank into the deepest depths of sin.

In 1748, at the age of twenty-three, he ran into a savage storm that threatened to carry him and his ship to the bottom. They say there are no atheists in foxholes during a war and perhaps it is equally true that there are no atheists on a ship caught in a vicious storm at sea. Newton thought of himself, like Jonah, as the cause of the mountainous waves and raging wind that threatened to engulf the boat and its passengers. This close brush with death set him thinking about the true meaning of life and led him to read at sea Thomas a Kempis's classic, *Imitation of Christ.*

The Holy Spirit used the storm and the book to convict him of his need of Christ. Sick of his pitiable condition and of the filthy slave business, he was led to leave the slave trade and ultimately to go into the ministry. All through his life John Newton never ceased to marvel at the grace of God that transformed him so completely. While pastoring his church in the town of Olney, he wrote his spiritual autobiography in a song that God gave him from the dark night of his soul.

Most people who sing his words about God's grace "that saved a wretch like me" do not feel that they have been "wretches." But that is exactly what John Newton realized he was when Christ saved him. Wherever he went to preach, large crowds gathered to hear the "old converted sea captain." He declared, "Had you known that my conduct, principles and heart were still darker than my outward condition — how little would you have imagined that such a one was reserved to be such an instance of the providential care and exuberant goodness of God." His testimony has resonated around the world in his beloved hymn:

> Amazing grace! how sweet the sound,
>   That saved a wretch like me!
> I once was lost, but now am found,
>   Was blind but now I see.
>
> 'Twas grace that taught my heart to fear,
>   And grace my fears relieved;
> How precious did that grace appear
>   The hour I first believed!
>
> Through many dangers, toils and snares
>   I have already come;
> 'Tis grace has brought me safe thus far,
>   And grace will lead me home.
>
> When we've been there ten thousand years,
>   Bright shining as the sun,
> We've no less days to sing God's praise
>   ·Than when we first begun.

The tune, so perfectly wedded to these words, is an early American folk melody, a plantation tune from the southern United States.

In his later years Newton joined William Wilberforce and other leaders in the crusade to abolish the slave trade in England. In the year of Newton's death, 1807, the British Parliament finally abolished slavery throughout its domain.

From his new life in Christ Newton also wrote, "How Sweet the Name of Jesus Sounds" and "Come My Soul, Thy Suit Prepare," along with many others. He set down his own epitaph, which today can be read on his granite tombstone:

> *John Newton, minister,*
> *Once an infidel and libertine,*
> *A servant of slaves in Africa,*
> *Was, by the rich mercy of our Lord and Savior Jesus Christ*
> *Preserved, restored, pardoned*
> *And appointed to preach the faith he*
> *Had long labored to destroy.*

Our spiritual biography no doubt is quite different and less dramatic. However, we are debtors to the same grace of God for saving us from sin and granting to us the blessings of his salvation. We echo Newton's testimony of amazing grace.

43 Since Jesus Came into My Heart

Written with a Pen Dipped in Pain

One would not surmise that the song of praise "Since Jesus Came into My Heart" was written with a pen dipped in pain. It is a shining example of the radiant promise tucked away in Isaiah: "I will give you the treasures of darkness, riches stored in secret places" (Isa. 45:3).

Herschel McDaniel was a promising young boy and the joy of his father's heart. But in 1913 he died at an early age and his father, Rufus H. McDaniel, was heartbroken.

In his bereavement Rufus McDaniel was led to rededicate his life to the Lord. He had not written any verse for several years, but in commemoration of the untimely death of his youngest son, he gave expression to the faith that sustained him in his dark night of loss and grief. The song was introduced during Billy Sunday's campaign in Philadelphia in 1915 and has since been sung around the world as a testimony of joy and trust.

McDaniel was led to praise God for the great work of grace in his life.

> What a wonderful change in my life has been wrought,
>   Since Jesus came into my heart;
> I have light in my soul for which long I had sought,
>   Since Jesus came into my heart.

> *Since Jesus came into my heart,*
> *Since Jesus came into my heart,*
> *Floods of joy o'er my soul,*
> *Like the sea billows roll,*
> *Since Jesus came into my heart.*

> *I have ceased from my wandering and going astray,*
> *Since Jesus came into my heart;*
> *And my sins which were many are all washed away,*
> *Since Jesus came into my heart.*

McDaniel witnessed in his song that the Lord who saved him was now the Lord who sustained him in his dark night of loss and sorrow:

> *I'm possessed of a hope that is steadfast and sure,*
> *Since Jesus came into my heart;*
> *And no dark clouds of doubt now my pathway obscure,*
> *Since Jesus came into my heart.*

Our hymnals usually omit a verse that for the author was a reason for his joy and praise even though his beloved son had gone through the valley of death:

> *There's a light in the valley of death now for me,*
> *Since Jesus came into my heart;*
> *And the gates of the city beyond I can see,*
> *Since Jesus came into my heart.*

Are you confronted with any "dark clouds of doubt"? There is "a hope that is steadfast and sure" for you. Has a loved one passed through the "valley of death"? If so, there is a light in that valley. It comes from the One who is the Light of the world. You can also with assurance sing with the author:

> *I shall go there to dwell in that city I know,*
> *Since Jesus came into my heart;*
> *And I'm happy, so happy, as onward I go,*
> *Since Jesus came into my heart.*

44 Through It All

Disappointed in Love

Andrae Crouch's vibrant spirit and songs have blessed the audiences at his sold-out concerts. One of his songs, though, was born in a time of deep disappointment. A young woman had joined his group known as the Disciples. She was a featured soloist and sang duets with Andrae. Soon he found that he was in love with her.

One Saturday she quit the group and left immediately to go overseas with another singing group. Andrae was devastated by her sudden and unexplained departure. He thought of canceling his coming engagements.

While in deep depression, he received a call from a close friend, who gave just the encouragement Andrae needed. After much prayer, and a sense of God's healing in his hurt and sadness, Andrae sat down at the piano and began playing a melody inspired by this experience. First came the tune, and then the words.

Three weeks later he prayed for inspiration to add a third stanza, and in the early morning of February 9, 1971, it came to him. Just as he finished writing it down, at five o'clock in the morning, the room began to shake as an earthquake rocked the San Fernando Valley, killing sixty-four people and causing a billion dollars of damage.

The song in the night that the Lord gave to Andrae Crouch can be your song and testimony in the dark night of your soul.

> *I've had many tears and sorrows,*
>   *I've had questions for tomorrow,*
>   *There've been times I didn't know right from wrong;*

But in every situation God gave blessed consolation
That my trials come to only make me strong.

Through it all, Through it all,
I've learned to trust in Jesus,
I've learned to trust in God;
Through it all, Through it all,
I've learned to depend upon His Word.

I've been in lots of places,
And I've seen a lot of faces,
There've been times I felt so all alone;
But in my lonely hours,
Yes, those precious lonely hours,
Jesus let me know that I was His own.

I thank God for the mountains,
And I thank Him for the valleys,
I thank Him for the storms He brought me through;
For if I'd never had a problem
I wouldn't know that He could solve them,
I'd never know what faith in God could do.

Are you facing some disappointment, some hurt, perhaps even an emotional or spiritual earthquake in your life? If so, find the strength and grace that comes from trusting in Jesus and depending upon his word.

45 Take the Name of Jesus with You

The Secret of a Pain-Ridden Life

Lydia Baxter lived with pain as an intimate companion, often bedridden for days at a time. She saturated her mind and soul with the word of God, which enabled her to know the joy of the Lord in spite of her great suffering. When friends came to visit they found that they were ministered unto by the buoyant spirit and faith of the one they had come to cheer.

"What is the secret of your sunny disposition when you are suffering so?" they would ask. Her reply: "I have the name of Jesus, and when the tempter comes to try to make me despondent because of my pain, I breathe the name of Jesus as my special protection from temptation. I mention the name of Jesus and the tempter can't get through anymore. When I feel badly, and wonder if I will ever enjoy a good night's sleep again, I take the name of Jesus, and ask Him to give me the soothing balm of His presence. He does and I soon drop off to sleep."

Lydia Baxter, born in 1809, came to know Christ as a young girl. After her marriage she and her husband moved to New York City, where they lived until she went to be with the Lord in 1874.

From her experience of how the name of Christ enabled her to surmount despondency and despair, she gave to others the song that has blessed and comforted so many.

> *Take the name of Jesus with you,*
> *Child of sorrow and of woe;*

It will joy and comfort give you,
Take it then where'er you go.

Precious name, O how sweet!
Hope of earth and joy of Heaven.

Take the name of Jesus ever
As a shield from every snare;
If temptations round you gather,
Breathe that holy name in prayer.

O the precious name of Jesus,
How it thrills our souls with joy,
When his loving arms receive us,
And his songs our tongues employ!

Of the over one hundred names and titles of our Lord, *Jesus* is the most endearing to his followers — the name by which we know him best. In the New Testament he is called by this name 909 times; over 500 times in the Gospels alone. The name *Jesus* means "Savior," designating his mighty work of salvation in our life.

When assailed by temptation, when despair seems to overtake us, let us breathe the name of Jesus, and find in our Savior the strength to overcome. The writer of Proverbs declares: "The name of the Lord is a strong tower; the righteous run to it and are safe" (Prov. 18:10).

Let us take the name of Jesus with us at all times, wherever we go, and find the power and peace that there is in that name. It is for each of us the "hope of earth and joy of Heaven."

46 There's Within My Heart a Melody

From a Calamitous Loss of Wife and Children

Luther Bridges, a successful young evangelist, accepted an invitation to hold two weeks of revival meetings near his wife's home in Horrodsburg, Kentucky, in 1910. His wife, whom he had met and married at Asbury College, stayed with their three boys at his in-laws while he conducted the meetings, at which many accepted Christ.

Near the end of the campaign he received a late-night phone call. The person at the other end conveyed the tragic news that his wife's parents' home had burned to the ground with his wife and three sons all lost in the fire. At the age of twenty-six he was bereft of his precious family.

Stunned and heartbroken he went to the word of God for comfort and guidance. In the storm that raged over his life God spoke to him, through the words of Psalm 91: "He who dwells in the shelter of the Most High will rest in the shadow of the Almighty. I will say of the Lord, 'He is my refuge and my fortress, my God, in whom I trust.'" That promise of God's word became an anchor for his soul. Like Job, he had suffered a calamitous loss, but his faith held firm.

Shortly after his tragedy he wrote and shared the song in the night that God gave to him from the deepened trust he found in Psalm 91:

There's within my heart a melody
Jesus whispers sweet and low:
Fear not, I am with thee; peace, be still
In all of life's ebb and flow.

Jesus, Jesus, Jesus,
Sweetest name I know,
Fills my every longing,
Keeps me singing as I go.

All my life was wrecked by sin and strife,
Discord filled my heart with pain;
Jesus swept across the broken strings,
Stirred the slumbering chords again.

Though sometimes He leads through waters deep,
Trials fall across the way,
Though sometimes the path seems rough and steep,
See His footprints all the way.

Feasting on the riches of His grace,
Resting 'neath his sheltering wing,
Always looking on his smiling face;
That is why I shout and sing.

Have you lost something or someone precious to you? Has some treasure of your life been snatched away? Has your heart been broken by a tragic circumstance that violently intruded upon the joy of your life? If so, listen, for God has a song in the night for you.

As promised through the Psalmist, God will be your shelter and your peace. "In all of life's ebbs and flows" God is there as Savior and Sovereign. He will "sweep across the broken strings" and give his melody of joy to the heart that trusts in him.

47 The Family of God

The Family in Time of Trouble

A young father was severely burned over most of his body in an explosion that ripped through the garage where he was working. Doctors told his family that he was not expected to live through the night.

Within an hour the members of his church in Anderson, Indiana, were alerted and a great prayer chain earnestly petitioned through the night hours for his recovery. The doctors reported that if he could make it through the next twenty-four hours he might have a chance.

Early the next morning, which was Easter Sunday, those who had prayed through the night learned that the man was still alive. Family and friends gathered for worship, heavy-hearted and tired from a sleepless night. At the beginning of the service the minister announced to the congregation that he had just spoken with the doctor, and the young man had passed the first crisis and had a good chance of survival.

The weariness of the long night gave way to praise and thanksgiving to God. Members celebrated the resurrection of our Lord with gratitude to God for this answer to prayer.

Among the members of that church were Bill and Gloria Gaither, the best-known gospel songwriters of our day, who have given us a rich repertoire of songs of faith. They, with other members of the congregation, were very moved that Easter Sunday by the prayer support of the church for the man whose life was endangered.

On their way home that Easter morning, they talked about the family of believers, the love and concern they had seen in action. Words and music started to be pieced together, their Easter noon meal having to wait. By the time they finally sat down to eat, one of the beautiful songs of our day was born, celebrating our being part of the family of God.

> *I'm so glad I'm a part of the family of God;*
> *I've been washed in the fountain, cleansed by His blood!*
> *Joint heirs with Jesus as we travel this sod,*
> *For I'm part of the family, the family of God.*
>
> *You will notice we say "brother and sister" 'round here —*
> *It's because we're a family and these folks are so near;*
> *When one has a heartache we all share the tears,*
> *And rejoice in each victory in this family so dear.*
>
> *From the door of an orphanage to the house of the King —*
> *No longer an outcast, a new song I sing;*
> *From rags unto riches, from the weak to the strong,*
> *I'm not worthy to be here, but praise God, I belong!*

Where is God when we suffer and go through trial? He comes and brings his grace to us through our brothers and sisters in the Lord. Christian believers are more than friends with each other. As this song, born out of a dark night of despair and danger, reminds us, we are family. We are bonded together in Christ.

Praise God, for he has joined us all together as members of his family. Let us uphold one another in prayer, love, and faith.

48 Jesus Loves Me

From the Story of a Dying Child

Karl Barth, the renowned Swiss theologian, one day was asked what he considered to be his greatest theological discovery. He replied: "Jesus loves me! This I know, for the Bible tells me so."

One Sunday at the close of a worship service at the Swiss colony L'Abri, Francis Schaeffer asked the congregation to sing "Jesus Loves Me." He smiled and added, "This is my favorite hymn."

Barth and Schaeffer would remind us that the most profound truths are usually the most simple. Indeed, there is no more sublime truth than that expressed by the words of this simple and beloved hymn. This song had a unique birth.

Two sisters, Anna and Susan Warner, lived near West Point, New York. They taught a Sunday-school Bible class in their home for West Point cadets. Between them, they wrote more than seventy books.

In 1860 they collaborated in writing the novel *Say and Seal,* which became a best-selling book of that day. In it, Johnny Fax, a young boy, suffered from a lingering disease. Near the end of the novel, Johnny asked his Sunday-school teacher to hold him and sing to him, as he often had done.

His teacher, holding the boy, started to make up and sing some simple words, "Jesus loves me, this I know." The plot of that novel, and this touching scene, gave birth to the now-famous hymn. The four stanzas appeared in the novel as a song of comfort for the dying boy.

This hymn has been sung by more children than has any other. It is considered to be the best-known hymn in the world, being translated by missionaries as a means of presenting the gospel in a clear, simple way. In 1861 William Bradbury composed the tune to which we now sing these words:

>*Jesus loves me! This I know,*
>>*For the Bible tells me so.*
>*Little ones to Him belong;*
>>*They are weak but He is strong.*
>
>>*Yes, Jesus loves me!*
>>*The Bible tells me so.*
>
>*Jesus loves me! He who died*
>>*Heaven's gate to open wide;*
>*He will wash away my sin,*
>>*Let His little child come in.*
>
>*Jesus loves me! He will stay*
>>*Close beside me all the way.*
>*Thou hast bled and died for me;*
>>*I will henceforth live for Thee.*

Jesus said, "Anyone who will not receive the kingdom of God like a little child will never enter it" (Luke 18:17). May we know the deep truth of these simple and beautiful words.

49 I Love to Tell the Story

During a Long Period of Recovery

On this early morning in my study, I write this article having just received word of the loss of a very close friend. To lose a friend is a great impoverishment, the loss of life's dearest treasure.

The bereaved husband called to share with us that his beloved had gone to be with the Lord. In the course of our conversation he added that someone had asked him during her illness, "Do you see the light at the end of the tunnel?" He had replied, "The light has been with us all the way. We have sensed God's presence and closeness through the people God has sent in our life who have been a source of strength and sustenance."

That is a statement of faith sounded in the depths of life that resonates with the radiant promises and presence of the God who gives songs in the night.

Katherine Hankey (1834–1911) was the daughter of a wealthy English banker. She cared deeply for people and early in life organized Sunday-school classes for girls working in the crowded factories and "sweat shops" of London. Her love for the "factory girls" led many of them to faith and several to become prominent Christian leaders.

Her zealous faith in Christ led her to prolific writings of Bible teachings and Christian verse. She donated all of her royalties to foreign mission projects.

At only thirty years of age she experienced a serious illness. During her long and painful period of recovery, God gave her a song in the night — a lengthy poem of one hundred verses on the life of Christ. From these verses came the text for two familiar and beloved hymns of the church: "I

Love to Tell the Story" and "Tell Me the Old, Old Story." God sanctified Katherine Hankey's suffering with songs that continue to bring blessing to many.

Our dear friend, who had told the story so eloquently by her life of beautiful service and often by her lovely voice, is now in the presence of the Lord she loved and served. And as this hymn affirms, she will now, amid scenes of glory, sing the new, new song of Jesus and his love.

> *I love to tell the story*
> > *Of unseen things above,*
> *Of Jesus and His glory,*
> > *Of Jesus and His love;*
> *I love to tell the story*
> > *Because I know 'tis true,*
> *It satisfies my longings*
> > *As nothing else can do.*
>
> *I love to tell the story,*
> > *For those who know it best*
> *Seem hungering and thirsting*
> > *To hear it like the rest;*
> *And when in scenes of glory*
> > *I sing the new, new song,*
> *'Twill be the old, old story*
> > *That I have loved so long.*
>
> *I love to tell the story!*
> > *'Twill be my theme in glory —*
> *To tell the old, old story*
> > *Of Jesus and His love.*

Is your life telling out the old, old story? Do you love to tell the story of Jesus and his love? There is no story in all the world that compares with it. Let us be faithful in telling it out to those around us.

50 I Have Seen His Face in Blessing

When a Loved One Suffers

Christians do not live in bomb-proof shelters, nor are they exempt from trouble. "A Christian is seldom long at ease,/When one trouble's gone, another doth him seize." So said old John Bunyan, and so it continues to be for the children of God.

William John McAlonan (1863–1925) found a dark valley of trial awaiting him in his pilgrimage of faith. While walking on a street in his native Ireland, he saw the strange sight of The Salvation Army in an open-air meeting. He stopped to listen. There was something about the gospel message from that outdoor meeting that he could not escape. Its seed had lodged in his heart and three months later he yielded his life to Christ.

Within two years he left his employment as a clerk and entered training for Salvation Army officership. After various headquarters appointments he served as territorial commander successively in Sweden, Switzerland, Germany, and Holland, then as an International Secretary and Director of the Army's Assurance Society.

The cloud that had been approaching over his horizon suddenly burst upon him in all its fury. A life-threatening illness struck his wife and sent her to the hospital, rendering her a horizontal citizen of the sickbed. For nine weeks she lay in the hospital and the doctor told her husband that she would not recover. She was released with no healing in sight, and although she later improved, she was unable to walk for some months afterward.

What greater trial is there than to see a loved one go through deep suffering and despair? It was during his wife's prolonged illness in the hospital and the bleak diagnosis that William McAlonan wrote the song that since has blessed many:

> *I have seen his face in blessing*
> > *When my eyes were dimmed with tears;*
> *I have felt his hand caressing*
> > *When my heart was torn by fears.*
> *When the shadows gathered o'er me,*
> > *And the gloom fell deep as night,*
> *In the darkness, just before me,*
> > *There were tokens of his light.*
>
> *I was wandering, and he found me,*
> > *Brought me from the verge of Hell;*
> *I was bruised, and he bound me,*
> > *Sick was I, he made me well.*
> *I was wounded, and he healed me*
> > *When a-wearied of the strife;*
> *I was erring, and he sealed me,*
> > *Dead, his Spirit gave me life.*
>
> *By his life's blood he has claimed me*
> > *As a jewel in his sight;*
> *As his own child he has named me,*
> > *Brought me forth to walk in light.*
> *So I'm fighting till he calls me,*
> > *Walking in the path he trod;*
> *And I care not what befalls me*
> > *Living in the life of God.*

Is someone dear going through a trial, a difficult period? If so, take heart, for you too may find in the darkness "tokens of his light." You are not alone. God cares and gives grace for the difficult times. Trust him and go on.

51 No One Ever Cared for Me Like Jesus

Healing from a Broken Marriage

The itinerant evangelist Charles Weigle (1871–1966) discovered one night after returning home from a preaching mission that his wife had left him. He found a note from her announcing that she had taken their little daughter and left, seeking a more glamorous life in a distant city.

Some time later, as she lay dying, she asked her daughter to try to "find your father and ask him to pray for me." But the message did not reach him in time.

Rev. Weigle experienced deep despair, even contemplating suicide. But through it all he claimed God's sustaining grace that saw him through.

One day, sitting at the piano, he pondered how God's love and care had sustained him in his dark night of sorrow. His fingers started to run over the keyboard, constructing chords and musical phrases. Then the song was born, the song that has brought comfort to many others who have known a broken heart.

The words, born out of heartbreak and despair, present a thumbnail biography of its author. From the heart that had been broken by sorrow, but healed by God's grace, there vibrated the chords for this song of assurance.

> *I would love to tell you what I think of Jesus,*
> *Since I found in Him a Friend so strong and true;*

I would tell you how He changed my life completely,
He did something that no other Friend could do.

No one ever cared for me like Jesus,
There's no other Friend so kind as He.
No one else could take the sin and darkness from me;
Oh how much He cared for me.

All my life was full of sin when Jesus found me,
All my heart was full of misery and woe;
Jesus placed His strong and loving arms around me,
And He led me in the way I ought to go.

Every day He comes to me with new assurance,
More and more I understand His words of love;
But I'll never know just why He came to save me
Till some day I see His blessed face above.

Many today know the pain of broken marriages, fractured families, despair in the tender relationships of life. Let us affirm the assuring truth that our Lord cares and understands, and will bring light in the darkness of our night. We should append to this hymn the apostle Peter's invitation to "cast all your care upon Him because He cares for you" (1 Peter 5:7).

VII FANNY CROSBY: QUEEN OF SACRED SONG

52 A Wonderful Savior

A Light out of Darkness

Fanny Crosby (1820–1915), America's most prolific hymn writer, authored more than six thousand hymns, blessing millions worldwide. Embarrassed by the volume of credits to her name, she used over two hundred pseudonyms. Fanny Crosby did her composing in a dark room — total darkness — for she was blinded in infancy by a doctor's mistake.

Her father died when she was a year old, requiring her mother to hire herself out to a wealthy family. When her grandmother heard that the little child was incurably blind, she said, "Then I will be her eyes." She took long walks with Fanny and graphically described the sunsets, clouds, trees, flowers, birds, and beauties of nature. Her grandmother's word pictures were so vivid that Fanny even had a favorite flower — the violet. She learned the sweet communion of prayer together with her grandmother as she knelt by her side.

Her grandmother also patiently taught her the Bible. With her phenomenal memory, Fanny committed to memory the first four books of the Old Testament, the four Gospels, the book of Proverbs, many of the Psalms, and favorite individual chapters, giving her a sound scriptural basis for her hymns.

Although she had no formal schooling, at the age of fifteen Fanny left home to enroll in the New York Institution for the Blind. There she became something of a celebrity, as she recited her poetry for famous visitors. She came to know every president in her time, except for Washington. She remained at the school for twenty-three years, eight as a student and fifteen as a teacher. She later became the first woman to address a joint session of Congress.

In her physical darkness God gave a light that radiated around the world through her beloved hymns. She expressed her testimony in one of her most popular songs, which includes, as do many of her lyrics, the word *see*.

> *A wonderful Savior is Jesus, my Lord,*
> *   A wonderful Savior to me;*
> *He hideth my soul in the cleft of the rock,*
> *   Where rivers of pleasure I see.*

> *A wonderful Savior is Jesus, my Lord,*
> *   He taketh my burden away;*
> *He holdeth me up and I shall not be moved,*
> *   He giveth me strength as my day.*

> *With numberless blessings each moment he crowns;*
> *   And filled with His goodness divine,*
> *I sing in my rapture: O glory to God*
> *   For such a redeemer as mine.*

This song reminds us that even though we may lose something precious we still have reason to rejoice in Christ and in his salvation for us. If Fanny Crosby, who never had earthly sight, could sing of a wonderful Savior and numberless blessings, how much more should we who see the beauty of the world and life around us praise God for his bounty and blessing.

53 To God Be the Glory

From the Night Watches

In her autobiography Fanny Crosby revealed, "Most of my poems have been written during the long night watches." At about ten o'clock she would retire to her room, close the door and quiet her thoughts. Then the inspired words would come, tumbling into her mind, sparkling with rhythm and images.

She would memorize her "songs in the night" until she could dictate them the next day. Her incredible memory enabled her to retain up to forty complete poems until they could be put on paper.

One of those songs from her night watches was featured in the 1954 Billy Graham Crusade in London. Soon Londoners were singing it on their way home — in the streets, while waiting for the bus, and on underground trains. Dr. Graham took it back to the United States, introduced it next in Tennessee, and saw it take its place among the favorite hymns of his worldwide crusades. Today an innumerable company lift their hearts in praise with her lyrics:

> *To God be the glory, great things he hath done!*
> *So loved he the world that he gave us His Son;*
> *Who yielded his life an atonement for sin,*
> *And opened the life gate that all may go in.*

> *Great things he hath taught us,*
> *Great things he hath done,*
> *And great our rejoicing through Jesus the Son;*

But purer and higher and greater will be
Our wonder, our rapture, when Jesus we see.

Do you also know something of "long night watches," when sleep will not come and darkness surrounds? If so, you too can contemplate the great things that God has done, has taught, and will yet do. That will awaken in your heart a song of praise in the night watches that will carry over to brighten the day.

54 Rescue the Perishing

A Song from the Slums

At the age of sixty, when many are planning retirement, Fanny Crosby launched out on a new career. She would spend several days a week in mission work in the slums of the Bowery district in New York City. Once after such a visit among the destitute and derelicts she returned home and wrote the now-famous hymn:

> *Rescue the perishing, care for the dying,*
> *Snatch them in pity from sin and the grave;*
> *Weep o'er the erring one, lift up the fallen,*
> *Tell them of Jesus, the mighty to save.*

> *Down in the human heart, crushed by the tempter,*
> *Feelings lie buried that grace can restore;*
> *Touched by a loving hand, wakened by kindness,*
> *Chords that were broken will vibrate once more.*

God gives a song, not only in our own night seasons of the soul but when we enter into the dark night of other lives. He often gives us his most precious songs as we serve him amid the hurts and heartaches of our world.

Just as Tolstoy's old shoemaker met Christ in the poor who came to his door, so we too will know his presence and his word to us through our concern and care for the perishing, the dying, the erring, and the fallen. Let us be about the people and places where the songs of Christ will resonate through the darkness.

55 I Must Have the Savior with Me

A Presence in the Darkness

Fanny Crosby scorned the idea that God planned her blindness. "The idea is repulsive to me that the Lord looked down on baby Fanny Crosby and ordained that she should be blind for life," she wrote in her autobiography. "I do believe that the Lord permitted me to be blind, when that affliction had been put upon me by a doctor's blundering, and I believe that the way has been shown to make my blindness a blessing."

She wrote further that she had prayed: "About being blind, Lord, there is something else I must tell you. At first I had a hard time dealing with it. And then I learned to accept it. And now something even better has happened. I thank you for it!"

She constantly leaned on the Lord's presence and grace to sustain her, as witnessed in her words:

> *I must have the Savior with me*
> *For I dare not walk alone;*
> *I must feel his presence near me,*
> *And his arm around me thrown.*
>
> *Then my soul shall fear no ill;*
> *Let him lead me where he will,*
> *I will go without a murmur,*
> *And his footsteps follow still.*

> *I must have the Savior with me,*
> *For my faith at best is weak;*
> *He can whisper words of comfort*
> *That no other voice can speak.*

> *I must have the Savior with me*
> *In the onward march of life;*
> *Through the tempest and the sunshine,*
> *Through the battle and the strife.*

When we surrender them to God, the tragedies that threaten to destroy or blight our lives become the source of our deepest understanding. Standing in the shadows, we may find God keeping watch over his own. We too, as Fanny Crosby, can have the Savior with us, and hear his "words of comfort that no other voice can speak."

56 Blessed Assurance

The Most Cherished Hope

At the age of eighty Fanny Crosby moved to Bridgeport, Connecticut, to live with her sister. There she increasingly thought of heaven and the blessings the Lord had in store for her. She anticipated for the first time having sight and expressed her most cherished hope in the confident refrain of one of her last hymns:

> Some day this earthly house will fall,
> And I no more as now shall see,
> But this I know, my All in All,
> Has now a place in heaven for me.
>
> And I shall see Him face to face,
> And tell the story, saved by grace.

Fanny Crosby received her sight one month before her ninety-fifth birthday, when that hope was realized as she opened her eyes in heaven. On her headstone is the verse of one of her most beloved hymns, "Blessed Assurance."

> Blessed assurance, Jesus is mine;
> O what a foretaste of glory divine!
> Heir of salvation, purchase of God,
> Born of His Spirit, washed in His blood.

Fanny Crosby has left us one of the great legacies of our faith — hymns that have endured and blessed for one hundred years, and still inspire and nurture our experience in Christ. Her ministry in verse is one of the greatest testimonies that indeed, "God gives songs in the night."

VIII SONGS OF PRAISE

57 Joyful, Joyful, We Adore Thee

A Majestic Melody out of Deafness

Joy is a hallmark of the Christian. The Founder of our faith said to his followers: "I have told you this so that my joy may be in you and that your joy may be complete" (John 15:11). Paul, the professor of our faith, reminds us that "the fruit of the Spirit is . . . joy" (Gal. 5:22). A joyless Christian would be a great contradiction.

Henry van Dyke (1852–1933), a famous preacher and writer of devotional material, when immersed in the beauty of the Berkshire Mountains was inspired to convey in verse this attribute of joy that marks the Christian life. The result was his celebrated hymn, "Joyful, Joyful, We Adore Thee."

The first stanza expresses joyful adoration to the "Giver of immortal gladness." The second has all of God's creation calling us to rejoice. The love of God provides the theme for the third verse and the final stanza invites all of God's children to join the mighty chorus of joy "which the morning stars began" (Job 38:7).

Henry van Dyke needed a tune that would convey the exhilaration of his words, while maintaining a dignity and worshipful mood. He realized that one perfect melody would express the joyful worship of his text — the final movement of Beethoven's Ninth Symphony, generally considered to be his greatest, which took him six years to complete. Beethoven combined both instruments and voices in a majestic expression of sound in what has become one of the world's premier musical productions.

But it is incredible to realize that its composer was stone deaf when he wrote this majestic melody. The Ninth Symphony premiered in Vienna and concluded with its magnificent choral ode to "Joy, thou heavenly spark of Godhead" — which to many represents the ultimate height that voices and orchestra can attain. Beethoven, standing in the midst of the rolling waves of sound, heard nothing. The soloists had to come down from the stage and turn Beethoven around so that he could recognize the thunderous applause he was being given.

Thus out of deafness has come to us one of the most joyful hymns of our faith, the perfect wedding of Beethoven's melody with van Dyke's words. Beethoven in his deafness, Milton and Fanny Crosby in their blindness, Joni Eareckson Tada in her paralysis, and a countless host of souls have heard celestial melodies in the night season that could never be heard in the brightness of day. Indeed, God gives some of his most glorious songs in the night seasons of life.

Let our souls exhilarate in the majestic praise of this great hymn.

> *Joyful, joyful, we adore Thee,*
> *God of glory, Lord of love;*
> *Hearts unfold like flow'rs before Thee,*
> *Hail Thee as the sun above.*
> *Melt the clouds of sin and sadness,*
> *Drive the dark of doubt away;*
> *Giver of immortal gladness,*
> *Fill us with the light of day!*
>
> *All Thy works with joy surround Thee,*
> *Earth and Heaven reflect Thy rays,*
> *Stars and angels sing around Thee,*
> *Center of unbroken praise;*
> *Field and forest, vale and mountain,*
> *Bloss'ming meadow, flashing sea,*
> *Chanting bird and flowing fountain*
> *Call us to rejoice in Thee.*
>
> *Thou art giving and forgiving,*
> *Ever blessing, ever blest,*
> *Wellspring of the joy of living,*
> *Ocean depth of happy rest!*
> *Thou the Father, Christ our Brother*
> *All who live in love are Thine:*

Teach us how to love each other,
  Lift us to the joy divine.

Mortals, join the mighty chorus
  Which the morning stars began;
Father love is reigning o'er us,
  Brother love binds man to man.
Ever singing, march we onward,
  Victors in the midst of strife;
Joyful music lifts us sunward
  In the triumph song of life.

58 How Great Thou Art

Inspired by a Thunder and Lightning Storm

Carl Boberg, a Swedish pastor, editor of a Christian newspaper, and member of the Swedish Parliament, was suddenly caught in a midday thunderstorm in 1886 while visiting a beautiful part of the coast of Sweden. The rolling thunder and flashing lightning filled him with awe.

Following the violent storm he was inspired by the calm water, the clear brilliant sunlight, and the sweet songs of the birds. The experience prompted him to fall to his knees in humble adoration of his mighty God. He penned his exaltation in the poem that later was translated into German and then from that into Russian.

In the 1930s Stuart K. Hine, serving as a missionary in a mountain village in Czechoslovakia, heard the song in its Russian translation. He translated the first stanza into English, also during a thunderstorm, then added the second and third stanzas as original work.

At the outbreak of World War II, Hine returned to England. In 1948 when refugees in England were desperate to return home, he wrote the fourth verse with its assurance that ultimately Christ will come to take each of us to our eternal home.

This twentieth-century hymn, sung to the tune of its Swedish folk melody, vaulted to popularity by its use in the Billy Graham crusades. In 1974 it was voted the number one hymn in America in a *Christian Herald* poll of its readers.

Let our hearts echo the praise and exaltation of this hymn for God's wonders of creation and grace.

O Lord my God, when I in awesome wonder
Consider all the worlds Thy hands have made,
I see the stars, I hear the rolling thunder,
Thy pow'r throughout the universe displayed!

When thru the woods and forest glades I wander
And hear the birds sing sweetly in the trees,
When I look down from lofty mountain grandeur
And hear the brook and feel the gentle breeze,

And when I think that God, His Son not sparing,
Sent Him to die, I scarce can take it in —
That on the cross, my burden gladly bearing,
He bled and died to take away my sin!

When Christ shall come with shout of acclamation
And take me home, what joy shall fill my heart!
Then I shall bow in humble adoration
And there proclaim, my God, how great Thou art!

Then sings my soul, my Savior God, to Thee;
How great Thou art, how great Thou art!
Then sings my soul, my Savior God, to Thee;
How great Thou art, how great Thou art!

Job, the arch sufferer, had endured his succession of calamities and the taunting of his friends. He longed for relief to his trials and for understanding of his undeserved suffering. The turning point in that classic book and in Job's life came when, as the text reads, "The Lord answered Job out of the storm" (Job 38:1). Job discovered the God who speaks to us in the storm, and that made all the difference.

God still speaks to us in the storms of life. His rainbow of grace will arch over the sky that has unleashed its storms upon us. Carl Boberg, out of a violent storm, found this great song of praise that has brought blessing the world over. Let us listen to and hear the songs that God gives in the storms of life.

59 All Creatures of Our God and King

Celebrating God's Creation

The beauty and wonders of nature eloquently declare the greatness and glory of God. St. Francis, one of the most fascinating figures in Christian history, saw all of nature as God's handiwork.

St. Francis was a mystic, a medieval monk who spent his lifetime as an itinerant evangelist, preaching and helping the poor people in Italy. His simplicity, devotion to Christ, and service to the poor have made him the only saint so recognized by all Christians and churches alike.

At the age of twenty-five, after an indulgent life as a soldier, he gave his life to God, turned his back on luxury, and sought thenceforth to imitate the selfless life of Christ in all that he did. He renounced his inheritance and all worldly ambitions to wed "Lady Poverty." He preached in the open air — at street corners, in the fields, and at public squares. He and his followers lived as the poor people among whom he worked.

"God's Troubadour," as he was known, celebrated God in all creation. He continually sang songs of praise. He sang to the birds, to the beggars, to the lepers, to the poor.

Near the end of his life, St. Francis entered into a night season. He became very ill and was suffering the loss of his eyesight. His celebrated paean of praise, one of our oldest hymns, was written in 1225 during this time of physical suffering, one year before his death.

Its stanzas call upon everything in nature to join in a great hymn of

146

praise to the Creator. This canticle of praise graces just about every hymn book today.

> *All creatures of our God and King,*
> *Lift up your voice and with us sing,*
> > *Alleluia, Alleluia!*
> *Thou burning sun and golden beam,*
> *Thou silver moon and softer gleam;*
> > *O praise Him! O praise Him!*

> *Thou rushing wind that art so strong,*
> *Ye clouds that sail in Heaven along,*
> > *O praise Him. Alleluia!*
> *Thou rising morn, in praise rejoice,*
> *Ye lights of evening, find a voice.*
> > *O praise Him! O praise Him!*

> *Thou flowing water, pure and clear,*
> *Make music for thy Lord to hear,*
> > *Alleluia, Alleluia!*
> *Thou fire so masterful and bright,*
> *That givest man both warmth and light.*
> > *O praise Him! O praise Him!*

> *Let all things their Creator bless*
> *And worship Him in humbleness;*
> > *O praise Him, Alleluia!*
> *Praise the Father, praise the Son,*
> *And praise the Spirit, Three in One;*
> > *O praise Him! O praise Him!*

Let us by our life and deeds praise our Creator.

60 My Redeemer

From the Wreckage of a Train

One of the joyful hymns we often sing is one that its composer never sang.

A train was en route to Chicago when a bridge near Ashtabula, Ohio, gave way and the train plunged into the icy river below. Fire broke out, immediately killing many who had escaped drowning but were trapped in the twisted wreckage. Only 14 of the 160 passengers survived.

Traveling on that train was Philip Bliss, thirty-eight years of age, returning with his wife from a Christmas visit in 1876 to his mother at his childhood home. Bliss survived the fall and escaped through a window. However, he returned to the wreckage in a frantic attempt to rescue his wife, and in so doing perished with her in the fire.

Bliss had made a profound and abiding impression upon the musical life of American Christendom. From his fluent pen had flowed such favorite hymns as "Almost Persuaded," "Hold the Fort," "Let the Lower Lights Be Burning," "Wonderful Words of Life," "The Light of the World Is Jesus."

Among his belongings in the train wreckage was found a manuscript on which Bliss had been working. The text became the popular and inspiring hymn, "My Redeemer."

> *I will sing of my Redeemer*
> *And His wondrous love to me;*
> *On the cruel cross He suffered,*
> *From the curse to set me free.*

I will tell the wondrous story,
How, my lost estate to save,
In His boundless love and mercy,
He the ransom freely gave.

I will praise my dear Redeemer,
His triumphant pow'r to tell,
How the victory He giveth
Over sin and death and hell.

I will sing of my Redeemer
And His heav'nly love to me;
He from death to life hath brought me,
Son of God with Him to be.

Sing, O sing of my Redeemer,
With His blood He purchased me;
On the cross He sealed my pardon,
Paid the debt and made me free.

Philip Bliss knew and served the God who brings triumph out of trials, symphonies out of suffering, and songs out of the darkest night. From the tragic loss of its author at the very height of his fruitful music ministry, and from the wreckage of a train have come the words now sung around the world.

61 Showers of Blessing

In a Prisoner-of-War Hospital

When Major Daniel Whittle left home to join the Northern Army in the American Civil War, his mother placed a New Testament in his kit. It remained there, unread. At the battle of Vicksburg the major lost his right arm and was taken prisoner by the Southern Army.

While recovering in the hospital, looking for something to read, he found the New Testament. He read it daily and was reminded of the faith he had been taught early in life but had forsaken. Still, his heart was not moved to accept Christ.

One night, Whittle was awakened by an orderly who said that a dying man in another room needed someone to come and pray with him. The major protested that he did not know how to pray or be of help. The startled orderly said, "But I thought you were a Christian; I have seen you reading your Bible."

Whittle finally consented to go with the orderly. The dying young man, seeing Whittle at his bedside, pleaded: "Pray for me. I was once on the right path when at home, but have strayed since I joined the Army. Now I am dying and I am not ready. Pray for me and ask God to forgive me."

Major Whittle later recorded his experience: "I dropped on my knees and held the boy's hand in mine. In a few broken words I confessed my sins and asked Christ to forgive me. I believed right there that He did forgive me. I then prayed earnestly for the boy. He became quiet and pressed my hand as I prayed and pleaded God's promises. When I arose from my knees, he was dead. A look of peace had come over his troubled face, and I cannot but believe that God who used him to bring me to the Savior, used me to lead him to trust Christ's precious blood and find pardon. I hope to meet him in heaven."

But for that little New Testament placed in a son's kit by a loving and praying mother, we might never have had the inspiring hymns "Showers of Blessing," "Moment by Moment," "I Know That My Redeemer Lives," and others.

From the barrenness and spiritual drought of his own life, in his dark night of the soul in that prisoner-of-war hospital, Major Daniel W. Whittle found, not drops of mercy but showers of blessing, which led to a fruitful life for God.

> *There shall be showers of blessing,*
> *This is the promise of love;*
> *There shall be seasons refreshing,*
> *Sent from the Savior above.*
>
> *Showers of blessing,*
> *Showers of blessing we need;*
> *Mercy drops around us are falling,*
> *But for the showers we plead.*
>
> *There shall be showers of blessing,*
> *Precious reviving again;*
> *Over the hills and the valleys*
> *Sound of abundance of rain.*
>
> *There shall be showers of blessing,*
> *Send them upon us, O Lord;*
> *Grant to us now a refreshing;*
> *Come and now honor Thy Word.*
>
> *There shall be showers of blessing,*
> *O that today they might fall,*
> *Now as to God we are confessing,*
> *Now as on Jesus we call!*

Is your life spiritually dry? Has life become barren, unproductive, in need of reviving, refreshing? If we seek God with all our heart, he will answer our prayer, open the windows of heaven, and send his showers of blessing upon us.

Let us claim for ourselves God's promise: "There will be showers of blessing" (Ezek. 34:26).

62 Sunshine in My Soul

Spreading Sunshine in the Darkness

Major Ruth Schoch has served at The Salvation Army mission station in Chikankata, Zambia, for twenty-seven years. There she has ministered to the most destitute, including those with leprosy and, more recently, those with AIDS. In that place of suffering, her life and spirit are a benediction to all who meet her.

Major Schoch is a shining example that when the sky above us may be overcast, when the shadows of life may surround us, we can have the sunshine of God within. Christ is the Sun of Righteousness, the Light of our life, and that makes all the difference.

Miss Eliza Hewitt of Philadelphia loved the outdoors, flowers, and nature. However, when she was a young school teacher she had an accident that left her a lifelong invalid. Confined to her room, she was denied the joy of the outdoors and the beauty of nature that she cherished. But through her Savior, the Light of her life, she wrote her witness in the now familiar hymn:

> *There is sunshine in my soul today,*
> *More glorious and bright,*
> *Than glows in any earthly sky,*
> *For Jesus is my light.*

> *There is music in my soul today,*
> *A carol to my King,*

And Jesus, listening, can hear
The song I cannot sing.

There is gladness in my soul today,
And hope, and peace, and love,
For blessing which He gives me now,
For joy laid up above.

Oh, there's sunshine, blessed sunshine,
While the peaceful, happy moments roll;
When Jesus shows His smiling face
There is sunshine in my soul.

Do clouds darken your sky? Do shadows lurk upon your path? Let Christ become the Light of your life, the Sun of your soul, and your life will be radiant with his presence and joy.

IX SONGS OF SERVICE

63 Brighten the Corner

In Confining Circumstances

Ina Ogdon of Toledo, Ohio, a talented speaker, was selected to travel with the prestigious Chautauqua Christian lecture team. She welcomed this opportunity to use her gift and reach thousands across the country.

Just before she was to leave on the tour, her father was seriously injured in an automobile accident. She canceled her touring plans to care for her father. Instead of travel and Christian teaching she took on the mundane duties of personal care and housework.

At first she felt anger and resentment. But gradually she found contentment and remained "true to the many duties near," "brightening the corner" where God had placed her.

Out of her night of the suffering of a loved one and her own sacrifice, Ina Ogdon gave to us the popular gospel song, "Brighten the Corner." Instead of speaking to thousands via the Chautauqua lectures, she touched millions through the words of her song.

> *Do not wait until some deed of greatness you may do.*
> *Do not wait to shed your light afar.*
> *To the many duties ever near you now be true;*
> *Brighten the corner where you are.*
>
> *Just above are clouded skies that you may help to clear;*
> *Let not narrow self your way debar.*
> *Tho into one heart alone may fall your song of cheer,*
> *Brighten the corner where you are.*

Here for all your talent you may surely find a need,
Here reflect the Bright and Morning Star.
Ever from your humble hand the bread of life may feed;
Brighten the corner where you are.

Brighten the corner where you are!
Brighten the corner where you are!
Someone far from harbor you may guide across the bar;
Brighten the corner where you are!

We may wish for a larger sphere of service, or to escape from confining circumstances. But just where we are God can use us. We may be the only light in someone's darkness. Let your light shine out for Christ, just where you are.

64 So Send I You

A Setting of Loneliness and Despair

Margaret Clarkson, born in 1915, is known for her hymns and her sixteen books, among them *Grace Grows Best In Winter*. At the age of twenty-three, she was isolated in a gold mining camp in northern Canada, far from family and friends. She experienced a deep loneliness — mental, cultural, and spiritual.

She records: "Studying the Word one night and thinking of the loneliness of my situation, I came to John 20:21, and the words 'So send I you.' Because of a physical disability I could never go to the mission field, but God seemed to tell me that night that this was my mission field, and this was where He had sent me."

She quickly set down her thoughts in a poem that was to become one of the most popular hymns on Christian service.

> *So send I you to labor unrewarded,*
>   *To serve unpaid, unloved, unsought, unknown,*
> *To bear rebuke, to suffer scorn and scoffing;*
>   *So send I you to toil for me alone.*
>
> *So send I you to bind the bruised and broken,*
>   *O'er wand'ring souls to work, to weep, to wake,*
> *To bear the burdens of a world aweary;*
>   *So send I you to suffer for my sake.*

So send I you to loneliness and longing,
　　With heart a-hung'ring for the loved and known,
Forsaking home and kindred, friend and dear one;
　　So send I you to know my love alone.

So send I you to leave your life's ambition,
　　To die to dear desire, self-will resign,
To labor long and love where men revile you;
　　So send I you to lose your life in Mine.

So send I you to hearts made hard by hatred,
　　To eyes made blind because they will not see,
To spend — tho' it be blood, to spend and spare not;
　　So send I you to taste of Calvary.

This great hymn, born in a setting of loneliness and of despair due to physical handicap, eloquently affirms that God has a work for each of us, whatever our circumstances. The late General Frederick Coutts, international leader of The Salvation Army, called for "men and women who are willing to pay the price of caring."

Let your life shine for Christ wherever you may be or wherever he may lead you.

65 Stand Up for Jesus

A Deathbed Challenge

A revival broke out in Philadelphia in 1858 under the powerful preaching of twenty-nine-year-old Dudley Tyng. Besides pastoring his own church he held noonday services at the downtown YMCA that attracted great crowds. On March 30 of that year over five thousand men gathered for a meeting during which Rev. Tyng preached from Exodus 10:11, "Ye that are men, now go and serve the Lord." Over one thousand of those present committed their lives to Christ. At one point in his sermon Rev. Tyng said, "I must tell my Master's errand, and I would rather that this right arm were amputated at the trunk than that I should come short of my duty to you in delivering God's message."

The next week, while visiting in the country, he was watching the operation of a corn-threshing machine in a barn. In those days donkeys were used to pull a long pole around in a circle, the pole attached to wheels that would grind the grain. Raising his hand to pet the head of one of the animals, a large cog caught his loose sleeve. In a moment his right arm was drawn into the cogs, lacerating it severely and severing the main artery. Four days later gangrene set in and the arm was amputated close to the shoulder. In two days, the shock to his system proving fatal, the young preacher went to be with his Lord.

A reporter recorded that on his death bed Tyng took his father's hand and said with much earnestness, "Stand up for Jesus, and tell all you meet to stand up for Jesus."

The next Sunday, Tyng's close friend and fellow worker, Rev. George Duffield, preached his morning sermon as a tribute to his departed friend.

His text was from Ephesians 6:14: "Stand firm then, with the belt of truth buckled around your waist." He concluded by reading a poem he had been inspired to write by the dying words of his co-worker. These words, later set to music, have been sung around the world as a hymn of challenge to Christians everywhere. In death, Dudley Tyng preached to a wider audience than ever he did in his lifetime.

> *Stand up, stand up for Jesus,*
> *Ye soldiers of the cross!*
> *Lift high His royal banner,*
> *It must not suffer loss.*
> *From victory unto victory*
> *His army shall He lead*
> *Till every foe is vanquished,*
> *And Christ is Lord indeed.*
>
> *Stand up, stand up for Jesus,*
> *The trumpet call obey;*
> *Forth to the mighty conflict*
> *In this His glorious day.*
> *Ye that are men now serve Him*
> *Against unnumbered foes;*
> *Let courage rise with danger*
> *And strength to strength oppose.*
>
> *Stand up, stand up for Jesus!*
> *Stand in His strength alone;*
> *The arm of flesh will fail you,*
> *Ye dare not trust your own.*
> *Put on salvation armor,*
> *And watching unto prayer,*
> *Where duty calls or danger,*
> *Be never wanting there.*
>
> *Stand up, stand up for Jesus!*
> *The strife will not be long;*
> *This day the noise of battle,*
> *The next the victor's song.*
> *To him that overcometh*
> *A crown of life shall be,*

He with the King of glory
Shall reign eternally.

Courageous people stand up for that which is important to them. They stand up for their rights. They stand up for their families. Soldiers stand up for their country, even being ready to sacrifice their lives in war.

A Christian is called upon to stand up for Jesus. May we with courage and an unfaltering commitment, in the time of testing, stand up and be counted for Jesus.

66 His Way with Thee

In Despair and Rebellion

Cyrus Silvester Nusbaum (1861–1937) was an evangelist in the Methodist Church. But even evangelists can become discouraged. He spent his first year as pastor struggling to care for seven congregations. He wrote: "It has been a most difficult task, strenuous and discouraging, and the income pitifully small."

He and his wife attended the annual conference, hoping and praying that he would be "appointed to a better charge." But he was appointed to the same difficult circuit.

In that dark night in his life, he sat up late, alone. He described his experience: "I was very unhappy and a spirit of rebellion seemed to possess me. About midnight, I finally knelt in prayer beside my chair. After some struggle, a deep peace came stealing into my heart. I told the Lord that I would be willing to let Him have His way with me regardless of the cost. With that feeling of surrender to the will of God, came the inspiration for the song, 'His Way with Thee.'"

> *Would you live for Jesus*
> *And be always pure and good?*
> *Would you walk with Him*
> *Within the narrow road?*
> *Would you have Him bear your burden,*
> *Carry all your load?*
> *Let Him have His way with thee.*

His pow'r can make you what you ought to be,
   His blood can cleanse your heart
And make you free,
   His love can fill your soul,
And you will see
   'Twas best for Him to have His way with thee.

Would you have Him make you free,
   And follow at His call?
Would you know the peace
   That comes by giving all?
Would you have Him save you,
   So that you can never fall?
Let Him have His way with thee.

Would you in His kingdom
   Find a place of constant rest?
Would you prove Him true
   In providential test?
Would you in His service
   Labor always at your best?
Let Him have His way with thee.

A discouraged evangelist, kneeling beside his chair at midnight, surrendered his despair and rebellion to God and found the secret to victory and peace. It was letting God have his way in his life.

Are you fighting a battle with some discouragement, some difficult circumstance, some inner rebellion? You too can find peace and power — by letting God have his way in that circumstance. In his will is our peace.

X SONGS OF LIFE
AFTER DEATH

67 Abide with Me

A Presence at Eventide

Henry F. Lyte (1793–1847), who pastored a poor parish church among fishing people in a coastal town in England, battled asthma and tuberculosis throughout his life. Despite physical frailty, he labored diligently and was greatly loved by his people. When admonished to spare himself, he coined the now well-known phrase, "It is better to wear out than to rust out."

His health worsened to the point where he was forced to seek out a warmer climate in Italy. It is recorded that he almost had to crawl to the pulpit for his final sermon in 1847.

Shortly before his move, weakened from the ravages of the lung disease and facing the pending sorrow of a permanent farewell from his beloved parish, he walked by the sea, this time with a very heavy heart. Soon he would be a stranger in a strange land.

By the seaside he watched the setting sun, realizing that his own life was ebbing to the close of "life's little day." In those sad moments he pondered the prayer and assurance of a manuscript that he was composing. He returned to his study to put the final touches on his poem, which became the immortal hymn, "Abide with Me." He gave the words to a friend who put it away in a trunk, where it lay for fourteen years. Lyte never made it to Italy, overtaken by death en route.

The poem was based on the gospel account of Christ's appearance to the two disciples on the road to Emmaus, and their request: "Abide with us, for it is toward evening, and the day is far spent" (Luke 24:29). Lyte wrote the words to be read, not sung.

The tune to which we sing Lyte's words, *Eventide,* was composed in just ten minutes, also in a dark night of the soul. William Monk (1823–89), wrote it while he himself was experiencing a deep personal sorrow.

Every believer is a traveler on the Emmaus Road. We travel that road, as the disciples of old, with our disappointments, our discouragements, and life's probing questions. The risen Lord still comes to his followers in need, to walk with us and talk with us along life's road of sorrows. He opens to us the glowing meaning of his word and his mighty work on our behalf.

The words of this song are essentially about death. The imagery of the ebbing tide of life is taken from the sequences of the passing day — eventide, deepening darkness, and fading glories. The song climaxes with the shadows fleeing before the breaking of heaven's morning. The last two lines of the song became the epitaph engraved on Lyte's gravestone.

Let us make the petition of this great hymn our own prayer and experience. Then we too will know the radiant presence of the risen Christ who will flood our prosaic path with his grace and glory.

> Abide with me; fast falls the eventide;
>   The darkness deepens; Lord, with me abide;
> When other helpers fail, and comforts flee,
>   Help of the helpless, O abide with me!
>
> Swift to its close ebbs life's little day;
>   Earth's joys grow dim, its glories pass away;
> Change and decay in all around I see;
>   O Thou who changest not, abide with me!
>
> I need Thy presence every passing hour;
>   What but Thy grace can foil the tempter's power?
> Who like Thyself my guide and stay can be?
>   Through cloud and sunshine, O abide with me!
>
> Hold Thou Thy cross before my closing eyes;
>   Shine through the gloom, and point me to the skies;
> Heaven's morning breaks, and earth's vain shadow's flee;
>   In life, in death, O Lord, abide with me!

68 In the Sweet By and By

Prescription from a Drugstore

Sanford Bennett (1836–98), a music teacher and instrumentalist, owned a drugstore in Elkhorn, Wisconsin. His friend, Joseph Webster, who had frequent bouts with depression, would often come to the store. Together they would compose songs that helped Webster come out of his melancholy.

One day Webster entered the drug store, obviously despondent. When Bennett inquired of the difficulty, Webster replied, "It's really nothing. It will be all right by and by." The reply sparked an inspiration. Bennett responded: "The sweet by and by. That would make a good hymn."

Sitting at his desk in the drugstore, Bennett wrote the words as they seemed to pour from his mind. He handed the sheet of paper to Webster, who brightened quickly. Webster reached for his violin, tuned it, and began to compose a melody for the hurriedly written lyrics.

In less than thirty minutes from the time Webster had walked into the store in a melancholy mood, he and Bennett, and two customers who happened to be in the store, were heartily singing the new song, "The Sweet By and By." It was published in 1868 and has since been a source of inspiration to many, often sung as a comfort at funerals.

> There's a land that is fairer than day,
> And by faith we can see it afar;
> For the Father waits over the way
> To prepare us a dwelling place there.

In the sweet by and by,
We shall meet on that beautiful shore.

We shall sing on that beautiful shore
The melodious songs of the blest;
And our spirits shall sorrow no more,
Not a sigh for the blessing of rest.

To our bountiful Father above
We will offer the tribute of praise
For the glorious gift of his love,
And the blessings that hallow our days.

Drugstores are places where people go for prescriptions for all kinds of maladies. This hymn was born in a drugstore as a prescription for depression. May its message of comfort and joy lift our spirits this day.

Our lives are so geared to this earth that we rarely think of heaven and what God is preparing for us. When discouragement would overtake us, let us look from the temporal to the eternal, from what earthly circumstances may inflict to what God is doing within and for us.

Let us remember that God is preparing what "no eye has seen, no ear has heard, no mind has conceived . . . for those who love Him" (1 Cor. 2:9). Take heart, our future is in his hands, and it will surpass our most daring dreams!

69 Nearer My God to Thee

Cradled in Sorrow and National Tragedy

The hymn "Nearer My God to Thee" was cradled in personal sorrow and had its maturing in an unusual history of both personal and national tragedy. The words express the heart's deep yearning, especially in times of trial and trouble, to be drawn nearer to God.

This hymn has come to be invariably associated with the ill-fated luxury ocean liner, the *Titanic*, which in 1912 struck an iceberg some sixteen hundred miles from New York City on its maiden voyage from England. As the few lifeboats pulled away carrying the six hundred passengers who were saved, all hope was lost for those left on deck. In the final moments as the ship slowly sank beneath the icy waters of the Atlantic, sending fifteen hundred helpless souls into eternity, survivors heard the ship's band playing the hymn's strains with passengers on board singing the words of one who had written them for her own comfort.

Sarah Flower Adams, author of the hymn, was born in England in 1805. Her mother died when she was only five. Her dream was to be an actress, and she began a successful career on the London stage, starring as Shakespeare's Lady Macbeth. But ill health forced her to give up her acting career, and she turned her talents to writing. Her health grew more and more fragile and she died at forty-three years of age.

The words of her hymn were inspired by the Scripture text of Genesis 28:11-17, the story of Jacob who, in deep distress, dreamed of a ladder reaching up to heaven. The words of the hymn recall Jacob's experience and the account's symbolic meaning to the pilgrim of God. Sarah

Adams expressed in the lyrics her faith that even in darkness and difficulty, we may be lifted nearer to God.

The hymn was the favorite of President William McKinley, who was assassinated in office. As he lay dying, he is said to have whispered its comforting words. On September 19, 1901, in every city of a saddened nation, citizens paused in silent prayer for five minutes and as a memorial sang the martyred president's favorite hymn.

> *Nearer, my God, to Thee,*
> *Nearer to Thee;*
> *E'en though it be a cross*
> *That raiseth me;*
> *Still all my song shall be,*
> *Nearer, my God, to Thee.*
> *Nearer to Thee.*
>
> *Though like the wanderer,*
> *The sun gone down,*
> *Darkness be over me,*
> *My rest a stone;*
> *Yet in my dreams I'd be*
> *Nearer, my God, to Thee.*
> *Nearer to Thee.*
>
> *There let the way appear,*
> *Steps unto heaven;*
> *All that Thou sendest me,*
> *In mercy given;*
> *Angels to beckon me,*
> *Nearer, my God, to Thee.*
> *Nearer to Thee.*
>
> *Then, with my waking thoughts*
> *Bright with Thy praise,*
> *Out of my stony griefs*
> *Bethel I'll raise;*
> *So by my woes to be*
> *Nearer, my God, to Thee.*
> *Nearer to Thee.*

We too, when experiencing the losses and crosses of life, can know the comforting presence and nearness of our Lord who promised, "Surely, I will be with you always, to the very end of the age" (Matt. 28:20). May the words of this great hymn be our prayer and experience.

70 Mansion over the Hilltop

Circumstances of Depression

While in his thirties Ira Stanphill (1914–93) penned the words, "You Can Have a Song in Your Heart at Night."

In later years he lived out that truth as he went through the dark nights of a broken marriage and his doctor's announcement, after discovering a malignant brain tumor, "You only have three months to live." He recovered and went on to write over five hundred songs, many during his times of trial and testing, proving God's promise that "he gives songs in the night" (Ps. 42:8).

In his preaching, Stanphill used the illustration of an industrialist who was facing bankruptcy. Depressed, he went for a drive and ended up in a poor neighborhood. Amid the rickety houses he saw a young girl who stood in front of the shack that was her home, her dress patched, clutching a tattered rag doll. Her smile and radiance contrasted strikingly to the grim poverty around her.

Curious, the man opened his car window and asked, "What makes you look so happy?" She exclaimed, "Because my father just inherited a fortune and he is building a mansion for us just over the hill."

The story sparked the tinder of his imagination and became an analogy for what the Lord is doing for his followers. In Jesus' farewell discourse to his disciples he had said, "In my Father's house are many mansions; if it were not so, I would have told you. I go to prepare a place for you" (John 14:2; NKJV).

Mr. Stanphill wedded the truth of that Scripture to the story of the little girl and gave us the song that has inspired the hope of believers for the eternal reward that the Lord has for his followers.

> *Tho' often tempted, tormented and tested*
> *And like the prophet, my pillow a stone,*
> *And tho I find here, no permanent dwelling,*
> *I know He'll give me a mansion my own.*

> *I've got a mansion just over the hilltop,*
> *In that bright land where we'll never grow old,*
> *And some day yonder, we will never more wander,*
> *But walk on streets of purest gold.*

> *Don't think me poor or, deserted or lonely*
> *I'm not discouraged, I'm heaven bound.*
> *I'm just a pilgrim in search of that city*
> *I want a mansion, a harp and a crown.*

Shortly before God's great soul winner and prayer warrior, Lt. Colonel Lyell Rader, O.F., went to his eternal reward, he wrote to his friends saying, "My bags are packed, I'm ready to go." When he temporarily recovered during his terminal illness he expressed disappointment to have found himself still on this side of eternity. In our world so preoccupied with the moment and with material things, we need that perspective of living — not for the temporal but for the eternal.

We follow One who has gone before and is preparing for us an eternal abode and inheritance that defies our most daring imaginings. Let us then press on that someday we may dwell "in that fair land where we'll never grow old."

71 Shall We Gather

Life at the River of Death

An oppressive heat wave afflicted the crowded city of Brooklyn, New York, in the summer of 1864. There was no air conditioning in those days. At the same time a deadly epidemic raged, leaving hundreds dead and dying in its wake.

Robert Lowry, a pastor in Brooklyn, visited his parish from house to house, comforting the sick and giving solace to the bereaved. He had often wondered why hymn writers had referred to "the river of death" but never to the "river of life" described in the Bible. As he visited families in mourning, he assured them that there will be a reunion by "the river of life flowing from the throne of God," taking his figure of speech from Revelation 22:1. He repeated this promise to hundreds of families from whom death had snatched a loved one from the family circle.

Returning late one day in July, weary from the oppressive heat and scenes of death and dying, he sat at his organ to give vent to his deep emotions. He thought of the many who had succumbed to the ravages of the epidemic — the little children as God's precious angels, the adults who had crossed over Jordan.

Lowry records that moment: "As I mused, the words began to construct themselves. They came first as a question of a Christian inquiry, 'Shall we gather?' Then they broke out in a chorus, as an answer of Christian faith, 'Yes, we'll gather.' On this question and answer the hymn developed itself." As the words and music began to flow, he soon was singing:

> *Shall we gather at the river,*
> *Where bright angel-feet have trod,*
> *With its crystal tide forever*
> *Flowing by the throne of God?*

He answered his question with an affirmation of faith:

> *Yes, we'll gather at the river,*
> *The beautiful, the beautiful river;*
> *Gather with the saints at the river,*
> *That flows by the throne of God.*

In one of the verses Lowry refers to what will be the crowning joy at the river of life: "They will see His face" (Rev. 22:4).

> *At the shining of the river,*
> *Mirror of the Savior's face,*
> *Saints whom death will never sever*
> *Raise their song of saving grace.*

What a glorious promise of God's word is enshrined in this hymn, inspired in the night season of death and grief. It speaks to us of the assurance that when traveling days here are done, there will be a gathering of God's people by the river of life. Those who have died in the faith, those whom "we have loved long since and lost awhile," will be there by that river of life. May we so live that we will gather with them at the crystal river that flows by the throne of God.

72 When the Roll Is Called Up Yonder

A Young Girl Is Called Home

A poorly clad fourteen-year-old girl, Bessie, the child of a drunkard, was sitting on the broken-down steps of a broken-down house in Williamsport, Pennsylvania. Professor James Black (1856–1938), a Sunday-school teacher, saw her there and asked, "Would you like to come to our Sunday school?" She replied, "Yes, I would like to go but . . ." Black answered, "I understand."

The next day he sent a parcel of clothing to the young girl, including a dress and new shoes. Bessie came that week and attended Sunday school faithfully for many weeks.

As president of the youth society Black would call the names of the members who answered the roll call by repeating Scripture texts. He always looked forward to Bessie answering to her name when the roll was called.

But one Sunday there was no response to Bessie's name. Thinking perhaps she had not heard, Black called her name a second time. Still there was no answer. He soon learned that Bessie had been suddenly taken ill and doctors held little hope for her. As he went home that day in 1893 the thought came to him that perhaps Bessie may never answer again.

Professor Black was a pianist and a published poet of note. Remembering Bessie, words started to flow through his mind about another roll call. He wrote them down, sat at the piano and composed the music, and this famous hymn was born. Black said that it all was written in about a half hour and he never changed a single word or note of what came to him in those minutes.

In just ten days Bessie died of pneumonia. The words that Black wrote before she went to answer the great roll call have spoken to many hearts through the years. It challenges each of us to be ready when "the roll is called up yonder."

When the trumpet of the Lord shall
    sound, and time shall be no more,
And the morning breaks, eternal,
    bright and fair;
When the saved of earth shall
gather over on the other shore,
And the roll is called up yonder,
    I'll be there.

On that bright and cloudless morning
    when the dead in Christ shall rise,
And the glory of His resurrection share,
When his chosen ones shall gather
    to their home beyond the skies,
And the roll is called up yonder,
    I'll be there.

Let us labor for the Master from
    the dawn till setting sun,
Let us tell of all his wondrous love and care;
Then, when all of life is over,
    and our work on earth is done,
And the roll is called up yonder,
    We'll be there.

73 Because He Lives

Assurance in Time of Difficulty

Bill and Gloria Gaither are the most prolific and famous husband and wife Christian song-writing team of all time. Their music ministry has been recognized with two Grammy Awards and dozens of Dove Awards, and nine times the Gospel Music Association has named them "Songwriter of the Year." Millions around the world have been blessed by their recordings, concerts, and over five hundred published songs.

One of their most famous songs was given by God in a night season of their soul. While expecting their third child the Gaithers were going through a difficult time. Misunderstanding troubled their church, Bill had a weakening and lingering bout with mononucleosis, and Gloria was apprehensive about the mixed-up world into which she was bringing her third child. For the Gaithers it had been a dry spell, as they had not written any songs for some time.

During this time of difficulty and darkness the Holy Spirit came very near with the calm assurance that "our child can face uncertain days because He lives." Their song, given by God in the night, has brought the radiant light of Easter truth to all of us who have sung its words of assurance.

> God sent His Son; they called Him Jesus,
> He came to love, heal and forgive.
> He bled and died to buy my pardon;
> An empty grave is there to prove
> My Savior lives.

Because he lives I can face tomorrow!
Because He lives all fear is gone!
Because I know He holds the future,
And life is worth the living
Just because He lives!

How sweet to hold our newborn baby,
And feel the pride and joy He gives;
But greater still the calm assurance:
This child can face uncertain days
Because He lives.

We cannot know what the future holds. Many ominous dangers lurk. But praise God, we know who holds the future. And that makes all the difference!

74 Beyond the Sunset

Blindness Transcended by Spiritual Sight

Virgil Block (1887–1978), a Quaker pastor, wrote more than five hundred gospel songs. He has left a record of the writing of his best-known hymn, "Beyond the Sunset," inspired by a beautiful sunset "witnessed" by a blind Christian:

"This song was born during a conversation at the dinner table, after watching a very beautiful sunset at Winona Lake, Indiana, with a blind guest — my cousin Horace Burr and his wife, Grace. A large area of the water appeared ablaze with the glory of God, yet threatening storm clouds were gathering overhead.

"Returning to our home, we went to the dinner table talking about the impressive spectacle we had witnessed. Our blind guest excitedly remarked that he had never seen a more beautiful sunset. 'People are always amazed when you talk about seeing,' I told him. 'I can see,' Horace replied. 'I see through other people's eyes, and I think I often see more; I see beyond the sunset.'

"The phrase, 'beyond the sunset' and the striking inflection of his voice struck me so forcibly, I began singing the first few measures. 'That's beautiful!' his wife interrupted. 'Please go to the piano and sing it.'

"We went to the piano nearby and completed the first verse. . . . Before the evening meal was finished, all four stanzas had been written and we sang the entire song together."

> Beyond the sunset, O blissful morning,
> When with our Savior heav'n is begun;

184

Earth's toiling ended, O glorious dawning —
Beyond the sunset when day is done.

Beyond the sunset no clouds will gather,
No storms will threaten, no fears annoy;
O day of gladness, O day unending —
Beyond the sunset, eternal joy!

Beyond the sunset a hand will guide me
To God the Father, whom I adore;
His glorious presence, His words of welcome,
Will be my portion on that fair shore.

Beyond the sunset, O glad reunion
With our dear loved ones who've gone before;
In that fair homeland we'll know no parting —
Beyond the sunset forever more!

Next time you see the spectacle of a sunset, see beyond it. Anticipate the glories of God's eternal tomorrow for the believer. For the person in Christ, the end of earthly time is eternity and the last step of life — beyond the sunset — leads into the presence and unending peace of God.

XI SONGS OF HISTORY

75 A Mighty Fortress Is Our God

Battle Hymn of the Reformation

The year 1529 was very difficult for Martin Luther. It was the darkest hour of his crucial movement. Sickness, despair, and danger beset him.

Twelve years earlier he had nailed to the cathedral door in Wittenberg, Germany, his 95 Theses (complaints) against the abuses of the Roman Church of that day, including the sale of indulgences that promised to get people out of hell if they gave money to help rebuild St. Peter's Church in Rome. That bold act ignited the Reformation, based on the tenets of the authority of the Scriptures, justification by faith, and the priesthood of all believers. For this Luther was excommunicated by the pope and burned in effigy.

Mired in depression, Luther turned to two of his most effective antidotes — music and Scripture. He wrote hymns, translated the Scripture into the common language of the people, and restored the practice of congregational singing. He even allowed the women to sing in public, a privilege that had been withheld from them for a thousand years. Often, when assailed by Satan, he would rid himself of his adversary with a song.

In that year of deep depression, Luther turned to Psalm 46. He repeated over and over again the first verse: "God is our refuge and strength, a very present help in trouble." Inspired by the strength he derived from that Psalm, he gave to Christendom one of his greatest legacies, the majestic "A Mighty Fortress Is Our God."

The hymn, inspired by God in Luther's night season, became the great rallying cry of the Reformation. It was sung in the streets. It was sung by the poor Protestant émigrés on their way into exile and by martyrs at their death. Its striking imagery summons all spiritual powers to the aid of the Christian under attack by Satan and his forces.

> *A mighty fortress is our God,*
> *A bulwark never failing;*
> *Our helper He amid the flood*
> *Of mortal ills prevailing.*
> *For still our ancient foe*
> *Doth seek to work us woe —*
> *His craft and pow'r are great*
> *And, armed with cruel hate,*
> *On earth is not his equal.*
>
> *Did we in our own strength confide*
> *Our striving would be losing.*
> *Were not the right man on our side,*
> *The Man of God's own choosing.*
> *Dost ask who that may be?*
> *Christ Jesus, it is He —*
> *Lord Sabaoth His name,*
> *From age to age the same —*
> *And He must win the battle.*
>
> *That word above all earthly pow'rs —*
> *No thanks to them abideth;*
> *The Spirit and the gifts are ours*
> *Thru Him who with us sideth.*
> *Let goods and kindred go,*
> *This mortal life also;*
> *The body they may kill:*
> *God's truth abideth still —*
> *His kingdom is forever.*

Through his writings, Bible translations, and hymns, Luther laid the foundations of a movement that forever changed the religious history of the world.

"A Mighty Fortress Is Our God" was sung at his funeral, and the first line of the hymn is engraved on his tomb at Wittenberg. This imperishable hymn, rugged like Luther himself, is one of the great classics of our faith.

We most likely will not know the same fierce opposition or have our life on the line as did Martin Luther. But we can know the same God as our refuge and strength, who will be for us "a very present help in trouble."

76 Now Thank We All Our God

A Table Grace in Time of War

When we sing the stately hymn of thanksgiving and praise "Now Thank We All Our God," we might not realize its birth in one of history's greatest periods of suffering.

Nothing brings more suffering and tragedy to our world as war. Even if one believes that war may be the necessary instrument for peace in some situations, it still leaves an aftermath of death and destruction.

One of history's longest and most terrible wars, the last of the great religious wars of Europe, was the Thirty Years' War of 1618–48. H. G. Wells described it as "one of the most cruel and destructive" of history. Germany, the main battleground between the warring Catholics and Protestants from various countries of Central Europe, suffered misery beyond description, with the German population decimated from sixteen million to six million.

At the outset, Martin Rinkart was called to pastor a church in the walled city of Eilenberg where many fugitives took refuge. He faithfully ministered to the sick and the dying of that city for the full period of the war, enduring the famines, plagues, and marching armies that swept through the city. During the dreadful plague of 1637, he would often conduct as many as forty funerals a day and ultimately over 4,500, including that of his wife.

Yet in the midst of the horrors of that war, Rinkart wrote a "table grace" that was sung as a national thanksgiving at the end of the Thirty Years' War. It became a hymn of praise sung across the centuries throughout the world, aided in popularity by its English translation.

The experience out of which this song was born reminds us that in the worst of circumstances, we can still raise our *Te Deum* in trial, our praise amid problems, and our doxology amid desolation.

Now thank we all our God
With hearts and hands and voices,
Who wondrous things hath done,
In whom this world rejoices;
Who from our mother's arms
    Hath blessed us on our way
With countless gifts of love,
    And still is ours today.

O may this bounteous God
    Through all our life be near us,
With ever joyful hearts
    And blessed peace to cheer us;
And keep us in His grace,
    And guide us when perplexed,
And free us from all ills
    In this world and the next.

All praise and thanks to God
    The Father now be given,
The Son, and Holy Ghost,
    Supreme in highest heaven;
The one eternal God,
    Whom earth and heaven adore
For thus it was, is now,
    And shall be evermore.

77 Once to Every Man and Nation

The Gathering Storm Clouds of War

This hymn was born out of the suffering caused by man's inhumanity to man as the clouds of impending war were on the horizon for the United States.

James Russell Lowell (1819–91) wrote the ninety-line poem "The Present Crisis" in 1845 as a protest against slavery and the war with Mexico. The hymn as we know it consists of sixteen lines excerpted from throughout the long poem and arranged by English hymnologist Garret Horder. It is the earliest American example of the social gospel represented in a hymn.

We are, individually and nationally, the product of our choices. Our decisions determine our destiny. We become what we choose to be in those moments when we make a choice between right and wrong, between excellence and expediency, between God's way and our own way.

The issues Lowell cites are ever with us. The "strife of truth with falsehood" makes the daily headlines. He challenges every generation with his famous lines, "Truth forever on the scaffold,/Wrong forever on the throne." But with the poet we affirm, "Yet that scaffold sways the future," for Christ is the Truth and he will ultimately triumph.

May our nation — and all nations — as this poem enjoins, choose good over evil, and have a courageous commitment to principle.

Once to every man and nation
Comes the moment to decide,
In the strife of truth with falsehood,
For the good or evil side;

Some great cause, some great decision,
Off'ring each the bloom or blight,
And the choice goes on forever
'Twixt that darkness and that light.

Though the cause of evil prosper,
Yet the truth alone is strong;
Though her portion be the scaffold,
And upon the throne be wrong.
Yet that scaffold sways the future,
And, behind the dim unknown,
Standeth God within the shadow,
Keeping watch above His own.

More than a century ago, the great French statesman and author Alexis de Tocqueville traveled extensively throughout the United States. He perceptively reported, "America is great because she is good. And if America ever ceases to be good, America will cease to be great."

May we each help America to be truly great!

78 The Church's One Foundation

Cauldron of Doctrinal Dispute

The history of the Christian church is far from idyllic. Rather, it is one of persecution and struggle, from its inception to the present day. Through the centuries the church has been attacked by those who would defile and destroy it with heretical doctrines or practices.

In 1866 an influential and liberal Anglican bishop attacked in a book the historic accuracy of the Pentateuch. A widespread controversy raged throughout the Anglican Church. Samuel J. Stone (1839–1900), a pastor ministering among the poor in London, was deeply stirred by the debate. He wrote a collection of twelve creedal hymns based on the Apostles' Creed, to instruct his people in the truth and to combat the liberal attacks on the Bible.

Stone knew that the foundation of the church must be the Lordship of Christ and not the views of people. His hymn "The Church's One Foundation" was based on the Ninth Article of the creed, which reads, "The Holy Catholic [Universal] Church; the Communion of Saints: He is the Head of this Body."

Thus from the cauldron of doctrinal dispute and crisis a century ago has come to us one of the great hymns of our faith. Stone's faith in the inspiration of Scripture, his refusal to compromise before the Higher Criticism of his day, and his conviction of the Lordship of Christ has given us this stately hymn.

> *The Church's one foundation*
> *Is Jesus Christ her Lord;*

She is His new creation
By water and the Word:
From heav'n He came and sought her
To be His holy bride;
With His own blood he bought her,
And for her life He died.

Elect from every nation,
Yet one o'er all the earth,
Her charter of salvation
One Lord, one faith, one birth;
One holy name she blesses,
Partakes one holy food,
And to one hope she presses,
With ev'ry grace endued.

'Mid toil and tribulation
And tumult of her war,
She waits the consummation
Of peace forever more;
Till with the vision glorious
Her longing eyes are blest,
And the great Church victorious
Shall be the Church at rest.

Yet she on earth hath union
With God the Three in One,
And mystic sweet communion
With those whose rest is won:
O happy ones and holy!
Lord, give us grace that we,
Like them, the meek and lowly,
On high may dwell with Thee.

May our individual lives be built on the foundation of Christ, the One who came and died and rose triumphantly. Then we may some day reign victoriously with him.

79 I Heard the Bells on Christmas Day

From the Despair of the Civil War

The Civil War was perhaps the darkest moment of despair in the history of the United States. Christmas came and the war and suffering seemed to mock the angels' song of "peace on earth."

In 1864 Henry Wadsworth Longfellow, out of that moment of despair, gave to us one of our most beautiful and eloquent Christmas carols. The poet's faith and hope strongly affirm that the peace and good will announced by the herald angels is still relevant, even in the midst of war.

> *I heard the bells on Christmas Day*
> *Their old familiar carols play,*
> *And wild and sweet the words repeat,*
> *Of peace on earth, good will to men.*
>
> *I thought how, as the day had come,*
> *The belfries of all Christendom*
> *Had rolled along the unbroken song*
> *Of peace on earth, good will to men.*
>
> *And in despair I bowed my head:*
> *"There is no peace on earth," I said.*
> *"For hate is strong and mocks the song*
> *Of peace on earth, good will to men."*

> *Then pealed the bells more loud and deep:*
> *"God is not dead: nor doth He sleep;*
> *The wrong shall fail, the right prevail,*
> *With peace on earth, good will to men!"*

As today in our world wars rage, famine stalks, and unrest and violence seem to prevail around us, let us listen again to the full proclamation of the angels. Many read about the peace and good will but forget that it is promised conditionally, to those who in faith accept the One who came in the miracle of the manger.

The full message announced on that night in the Judean hills was:

> *Glory to God in the highest,*
> *And on earth peace to men*
> *on whom his favor rests.*

The peace of which the angels sang does not deal with external circumstances around us. Rather, it is the peace that Christ gives within the heart when we know him as Savior and Lord. Let us know that true peace — peace of mind and heart that is a special gift of the Christ of Christmas.

80 Faith of Our Fathers

Remembering the Martyrs

This famous hymn conjures images of martyrs who through the centuries have suffered in chains and dungeons, by fire and sword. It should also call to mind the more recent persecution of believers in today's totalitarian countries. Some writers have indicated that more Christians have suffered persecution and martyrdom in this generation than in any other in history.

When Frederick W. Faber (1814–1863), an Anglican minister in England, penned these words, he was referring to those who were martyred during the reign of Henry VIII. One observer of that time wrote that the king "was butchering martyrs, including the most illustrious of his subjects, Thomas More."

We are all debtors to the innumerable company who have paid the ultimate cost of discipleship. The very Bible we are privileged to read rose as a phoenix out of the dungeons and fires of martyrdom.

The Salvation Army has not been without its heroes and heroines of the faith. Our movement was cradled in the swaddling clothes of sacrifice and persecution. The pioneers of the Army suffered great opposition and often violence. William Booth once said, "It's our troubles that give us our anecdotes."

Those familiar with our history will quickly call to mind stalwarts within the ranks who paid a high cost for fidelity to Christ. Major Yin Hung-shun, O.F., endured fifteen years in a labor camp in China. Brigadier Josef Korbel, O.F., was imprisoned for over ten years in Czechoslovakia. Major Noh Yong Soo was executed by the communists in Korea. Commissioner Stanley Cottrill and others suffered the ravages of a concentration camp in World War II. Two young women were murdered at The Salvation Army's Usher Institute in Zimbabwe. These, with many others, belong on the Army's Roll of Heroes.

Someone has expressed a profound truth in the ditty: "They entered Heaven by toil, tears and pain;/We pray, 'God give us grace to travel by the train.'"

Frederick Faber pondered the cruel persecutions and martyrdoms that took place during the sixteenth century and in his own day. From that dark night of church history he wrote the hymn "Faith of Our Fathers," to remind those of his day of the heritage that was theirs and to encourage their fidelity under persecution.

> *Faith of our fathers, living still*
> *In spite of dungeon, fire and sword,*
> *O how our hearts beat high with joy*
> *Whene'er we hear that glorious word!*
>
> *Faith of our fathers, holy faith,*
> *We will be true to Thee till death.*
>
> *Faith of our fathers, faith and prayer,*
> *Have kept our country brave and free,*
> *And through the truth that comes from God,*
> *Her children have true liberty.*

May we be true to the faith of our fathers and of our mothers, and of all those who have left us such a treasured heritage.

81 We Gather Together

Thanksgiving out of the Oppression of War

The author of this text is not known, but the historical setting is that of a great struggle for political and religious freedom near the end of the sixteenth century. The hymn celebrates the freedom of the Dutch from the oppressive rule of Spain, when Holland's cities were captured and sacked by Spanish armies and its Protestant citizens exiled.

Out of the oppression and trials of war has come this traditional Thanksgiving hymn:

> *We gather together*
> > *To ask the Lord's blessing.*
> *He chastens and hastens*
> > *His will to make known.*
> *The wicked oppressing*
> > *Now cease from distressing.*
> *Sing praises to His name —*
> > *He forgets not His own.*

> *Beside us to guide us,*
> > *Our God with us joining,*
> *Ordaining, maintaining*
> > *His kingdom divine;*
> *So from the beginning*

The fight we were winning:
Thou, Lord, wast at our side —
All glory be Thine.

We all do extol Thee,
Thou leader triumphant
And pray that Thou still
Our Defender wilt be;
Let Thy congregation
Escape tribulation:
Thy name be ever praised!
O Lord, make us free!

May our Thanksgiving season be something more than a time of feasting and festivities. Let us thank God for his blessing upon our nation and the cherished freedom that is ours. Let us pray that God may be "beside us to guide us." Let us with families and friends, and with God's people, "gather together to ask the Lord's blessing."

82 America the Beautiful

Our Heritage of Freedom

This patriotic hymn grew out of the author's two exceptional encounters with the beauty of art and nature, which spoke to her of God's grace for America.

In 1893 Katharine Lee Bates (1859–1929), a thirty-four-year-old professor of English from Wellesley College, en route to Colorado, stopped off to see the "White City" at the Columbian Exposition in Chicago, which over several years was celebrating the 400th anniversary of the discovery of America. She recorded: "The White City made such strong appeal to patriotic feeling that it was in no small degree responsible for at least the last stanza of 'America the Beautiful.' It was with this quickened and deepened sense of America that we traveled farther west, my New England eyes delighting in the wind-waved gold of the vast wheat-fields."

The second experience was Miss Bates' ascent of Pike's Peak, Colorado. The view from this fifteen-thousand-foot summit with its breathtaking panorama led her to ponder the magnificent endowment of God upon America, and inspired her to pencil in her notebook the four stanzas of the poem. The majestic scene became compressed by the poet into such sparkling phrases as "spacious skies," "amber waves of grain," "purple mountain majesties," and "fruited plains."

But the hymn also recognizes the background of struggle and sacrifice that stir us to an appreciation of the country's heritage. The night seasons of our nation's history and heritage permeate the hymn. The "pilgrim feet" were those that trekked across the mountains and the Great Plains and endured the hardness and struggle that founded the nation.

"Stern" is her word for the hardships of an untamed land that they had to overcome. "Impassioned stress" speaks of the quest and struggle for freedom. "Liberating strife" recalls Bunker Hill, Valley Forge, Gettysburg.

This noble hymn closes each stanza with a deep yearning prayer for God to grant the higher gifts to America — to mend its flaws, refine its gold, give self-control and liberty in law, and to crown its good with brotherhood. The author felt deeply about the message of her patriotic hymn and wrote, "We must match the greatness of our country with the goodness of personal godly living."

On her memorable trip Katharine Bates understood something more than her impression of the greatness and vastness of America. She said, "Greatness and goodness are not necessarily synonymous. Rome was great, but she was not good, and for that reason the Roman Empire fell. . . . Unless we are willing to crown our greatness with goodness, and our bounty with brotherhood, our beloved America may go the same way."

The hymn attained widespread popularity during the difficult days of World War I, fostering patriotic pride and prayer throughout the nation. Then in the summer of 1960 the United States launched its first communications satellite, Echo I, orbiting a thousand miles above the earth. Received and relayed back to the United States was the first music used in the new space-age communications system. The words listeners heard were those of "O Beautiful for Spacious Skies."

May this hymn remind us that America owes its birth and greatness to a faith in God. Today there is a need to return to a national dependence upon God as well as a renewed pride in America the Beautiful. Let our hearts echo the prayers of this great hymn, that America will be a nation of righteousness, of self-control, of liberty within law, and that God will "crown [that] good with brotherhood from sea to shining sea."

> O beautiful for spacious skies,
>   For amber waves of grain,
> For purple mountain majesties
>   Above the fruited plain!
> America! America!
>   God shed His grace on thee.
> And crown thy good with brotherhood
>   From sea to shining sea.
>
> O beautiful for pilgrim feet,
>   Whose stern, impassioned stress

A thoroughfare for freedom beat
    Across the wilderness!
America! America!
    God mend thine ev'ry flaw,
Confirm thy soul in self-control,
    Thy liberty in law.

O beautiful for heroes proved
    In liberating strife,
Who more than self their country loved,
    And mercy more than life!
America! America!
    May God thy gold refine
Till all success be nobleness
    And every gain divine!

O beautiful for patriot dream
    That sees beyond the years,
Thine alabaster cities gleam —
    Undimmed by human tears!
America! America!
    God shed His grace on thee,
And crown thy good with brotherhood
    From sea to shining sea.

XII SONGS IN THE BIBLE

83 Great Is Thy Faithfulness

From the Saddest Book in the Bible

The saddest book in the Bible is Lamentations. Its very name means a weeping or wailing in grief. Lamentations is Jeremiah's mournful cry of anguish over the sufferings of Judah and Jerusalem. Destroyed and desolate, Jerusalem is personified as a lonely widow: "How deserted lies the city, once so full of people! How like a widow is she, who once was great among the nations!" (1:1).

Her crown of sorrows is remembering happier days: "All the splendor has departed from the Daughter of Zion. . . . In the days of her affliction and wandering Jerusalem remembers all the treasures that were hers in days of old" (1:6-7). Her plaintive cry longs for sympathy: "Is it nothing to you, all you who pass by? Look around and see. Is any suffering like my suffering?" (1:12).

In the midst of this incomparable dirge with its tears and terrors comes one of the brightest jewels of the Bible: "For his compassions never fail. They are new every morning; great is your faithfulness" (3:22-23). Here in this dark night of a nation's soul God gives one of his most radiant songs.

This textual jewel inspired Thomas Chisholm to write the song that has blessed an innumerable company with the truth of this golden text:

> Great is thy faithfulness, O God my Father,
> There is no shadow of turning with thee;
> Thou changest not, thy compassions they fail not;
> As thou has been thou forever wilt be.

Great is thy faithfulness!
Great is thy faithfulness!
Morning by morning new mercies I see;
· All I have needed Thy hand hath provided;
Great is thy faithfulness, Lord, unto me!

Summer and winter, and springtime and harvest,
Sun, moon and stars in their courses above,
Join with all nature in manifold witness
To thy great faithfulness, mercy and love.

Pardon for sin and a peace that endureth,
Thy own dear presence to cheer and to guide;
Strength for today and bright hope for tomorrow,
Blessings all mine, with ten thousand beside!

Let us remember this golden truth, that God is faithful and his compassion will never fail us. The faithfulness of God is an unfailing anchor for each of us on our storm-tossed sea of life.

84 There Is a Balm in Gilead

From a Nation's Suffering

Smitten with remorseless grief for his people's incomparable suffering, Jeremiah cries out: "Is there no balm in Gilead? Is there no physician there? Why then is there no healing for the wound of my people?" (Jer. 8:22).

Gilead had long been known for its balm, made from the resin of the mastic tree and used by physicians of the Eastern world. If there were no balm in Gilead, then there would be no hope for their healing.

Indeed, there was "no balm in Gilead" that could cure their soul sickness. The people's obstinacy made it a sickness unto death.

But, in light of the New Testament and Calvary, the piercing pathos of the prophet's question has been answered in the traditional spiritual of the slave-poets. With intense feeling and profound conviction they responded to Jeremiah's despairing queries that Jesus does heal the sin-sick soul.

> *Sometimes I feel discouraged,*
> *   And think my work's in vain.*
> *But then the Holy Spirit*
> *   Revives my soul again.*

> *There is a balm in Gilead*
> *   To make the wounded whole;*
> *There is a balm in Gilead*
> *   To heal the sin-sick soul.*

> *If you can't preach like Peter,*
> *If you can't pray like Paul,*
> *Just tell the love of Jesus,*
> *And say He died for all.*

The truth of this song that had its inspiration in the cauldron of Israel's suffering in Old Testament times found new expression in the deep suffering of the slaves in America. Its enduring message reminds us that our Lord is still the Great Physician who "makes the wounded whole" and "heals the sin-sick soul."

If you have been wounded in life, or if you have a soul sickness, look to Christ who alone brings healing and wholeness. The Psalmist eloquently declares his healing power: "Who forgives all your iniquities, Who heals all your diseases, Who redeems your life from destruction, Who crowns you with lovingkindness and tender mercies" (Ps. 103:3-4).

85 Paul and Silas in Prison

Midnight in the Dungeon

What would you do if you were unjustly thrown into prison? Some would grumble, growl, grouch, grouse, and gripe. Others would fume and fuss, moan and groan.

Paul and Silas were not only cast into prison but were "stripped and beaten and severely flogged." They yearned to preach the Gospel. Instead, they are in solitary confinement — beaten and bloody, their feet fastened in tortuous stocks. What could they do?

The account reads: "About midnight Paul and Silas were praying and singing hymns to God, and the other prisoners were listening to them" (Acts 16:25). Why were death-row inmates singing praises instead of the blues? Because God gave them a song that turned them into a duo with a duet in their dungeon. God was the "choir director" that night who provided the sheet music for his two midnight minstrels. Paul and Silas had learned with afflicted Job that "God gives songs in the night."

Luke tells us that "the other prisoners were listening to them." Imagine the hymns resonating down those prison corridors and into each cell! Imagine being able to sing in prison!

The record tells us that it was "about midnight." When you are in excruciating pain, it is not an easy thing to sing a song at midnight. For these two men of God, in their darkest hour, God put a song in their hearts and upon their lips.

This chapter of Scripture gives us one of the most beautiful and dramatic accounts of conversion in the Bible. Suddenly the whole prison was rocked by an earthquake. "The foundations of the prison were shaken. At once all the prison doors flew open, and everybody's chains came loose."

The jailer, horrified to think that his charges had escaped, a capital offense in Rome, was about to commit suicide. But Paul shouted, "Don't harm yourself! We are all here!"

"The jailer called for lights, rushed in and fell trembling before Paul and Silas. He then brought them out and asked, 'Sirs, what must I do to be saved?'

"They replied, 'Believe in the Lord Jesus, and you will be saved — you and your household.'" We read that Paul and Silas then shared the word of God with the jailer and his family. "At that hour of the night the jailer took them and washed their wounds; then immediately he and all his family were baptized. The jailer brought them into his house and set a meal before them, and the whole family was filled with joy, because they had come to believe in God" (Acts 16:22-34).

This story is a memorial to God's provision of a song in the most painful and difficult of circumstances. In their dark dungeon, as these two missionaries prayed and praised God in song, the gloom around them was dispelled.

Are you in dark and difficult circumstances? Whatever your condition, if you pray with a sincere heart, you will find that God gives a song in the night.

Let us find that song and lift our hearts in prayer and praise to him. We too may find that he will change our darkness into light, our suffering into singing, and our problems into praise.

86 I Know That My Redeemer Lives

Job's Song in the Night

Job suffered the severest calamities of anyone in the Bible. His whole world came tumbling down as he lost his possessions, his family, his health, and the respect of his peers.

From the pages that record the unequaled sufferings of Job emerges one of the most radiant promises of the Bible: "God . . . gives songs in the night" (35:10). Job knew well this beautiful providence of God. When the curtain of catastrophe fell over his soul, a shaft of brilliant sunlight broke through his black sky and God gave him the sublime song, "I know that my Redeemer lives!"

Job's song in the night is the most radiant text on immortality in the Old Testament. From his pit of futility Job rises to his pinnacle of faith, as described in the most memorable passage of this noble book. A shaft of brilliant sunlight breaks through the dark clouds that overshadow him and he exclaims:

> I know that my Redeemer lives, And that in the end he will stand upon the earth, And after my skin has been destroyed, yet in my flesh I will see God. I myself will see him with my own eyes — I, and not another. How my heart yearns within me! (19:25-27)

Handel caught the immortal cadences and set it to the stirring soprano strains of his *Messiah*. This composition, perhaps the greatest single piece of Christian music, has sung its way into hearts around the world. Job's song in the night, given to him by God, resonates across the millenniums to our living rooms and hearts. We hear and thrill to its staunch affirmation each Advent and Easter season.

From the Old Testament book of deepest darkness has come the song of most radiant light! From the Old Testament's greatest tragedy comes the song of grandest triumph! God turns our sorrows into symphonies!

"I know" is the affirmation of Job. He did not say, "I hope" or "I think." He declared, "I know." There need be no equivocation on this central issue of our lives. We too can know that Christ lives and, as Job, can know him as "my" Redeemer.

With inspired foresight Job anticipates centuries in advance our Lord's coming to earth, the supreme event of history. Job exclaims of his desire to behold the Lord, "How my heart yearns within me." If Job, in the misty dawn of history, could express this yearning, how much more should we — who have known his mighty life, his infinite sacrifice, his unfailing love and grace. May we have a deep yearning for that day when our eyes shall behold our Savior and the Lord of glory. It will be the supreme event of our lives.

Job was but the forerunner of the great company to whom God would give songs in the night. We of the Christian era, who are children of the Resurrection, can live with this great affirmation, realization, and anticipation of the risen Christ.

Are you going through a night season? Have dark shadows fallen across your pathway? Listen, God has a song in the night for you. And the transforming truth of Job's song, that can be your song, will make all the difference for time and eternity.

XIII SONGS OF AN ARMY

87 My Life Must Be Christ's Broken Bread

In the Aftermath of War

Only a little over fifty years ago, World War II claimed the lives of fifty million persons, wounded tens of millions more, and spread death and destruction across six of the world's seven continents and all of its oceans. The world became sharply divided and many countries and peoples paid a horrible price.

A serious question back then had to be, "Can the internationalism of The Salvation Army survive such a terrible rupture in world relations?"

England and Germany were arch enemies during the bitter war years. Shortly after the war, General Albert Orsborn, an Englishman and leader of the international Salvation Army, went to Germany to meet with German Salvationists.

Orsborn saw the destruction wreaked upon Hamburg and Berlin. He saw his comrade German Salvationists, whose country had been so devastated, in their tattered uniforms, and wondered how he could bridge the great gulf between himself and them.

When I was privileged to interview General Orsborn in his home in retirement in 1966, he shared the story of a great song that was born in the aftermath of war.

"Soon after I was elected in 1946 I went to Berlin. I went there, thinking to myself, now how can I possibly reach these people, these German Salvationists? Not long ago, we were supposed to be political enemies and now I am here as the international leader of The Salvation Army and they are receiving me, and looking to me and listening to me, and hoping that I can bring them some inspiration. How can I leap over the political gulf that has been created in these cruel war years? How can I make them feel what I want them to feel about the Kingdom and about our work?

"Here am I, in a fine uniform — true, my second best and not my very best, because I was sensitive about my appearance before the German officers. And, there are they, with worn uniforms — patched and altered as best they could. And the women with bonnets which had very evidently been renewed for this special occasion. And as some of the men knelt in prayer, I noticed the soles of their boots were worn through. So, I said to myself, how can I get over this gulf between us, this tremendous difference in our living conditions?

"Then I went to my billet in the Red Shield Hostel in Berlin. And still, in some anxiety, I knelt by my bed. And as I knelt there, the first verse of this song formed itself in my mind.

"Now I believe that these songs, these spiritual songs, are the work of the Holy Spirit. The writers are His instruments. It is the business of the writer to listen in and to keep his mind and heart attuned to the work of the Holy Spirit. And then, maybe, he will catch the immortal cadences. Then perhaps he will hear something that is not ordinarily heard by men who are preoccupied with earthly concerns.

"So I prayed and I waited and then the first verse came:

> *My life must be Christ's broken bread,*
> *My love His outpoured wine,*
> *A cup o'erfilled, a table spread*
> *Beneath His name and sign,*
> *That other souls, refreshed and fed*
> *May share His life through mine.*

"I had to go to the officers' meeting, but I felt a new spirit surging within me and God came graciously near to us and blessed us and brought us truly together in that spirit of unity which is the work of the Holy Ghost.

"I went on to Holland and, as I went, I wrote in the car. My companion, Colonel Dalziel, was too wise to interrupt me. He knew what I was doing. So I wrote the second verse on Hitler's Autobahn between Berlin and Holland, and the third verse when I reached home.

> *My all is in the Master's hands*
> *For Him to bless and break;*

Beyond the brook His winepress stands
And thence my way I take,
Resolved the whole of love's demands
To give, for His dear sake.

Lord, let me share that grace of Thine
Wherewith Thou didst sustain
The burden of the fruitful vine,
The gift of buried grain.
Who dies with Thee, O Word divine,
Shall rise and live again.

"Now this song has been made a great blessing. It has gone far outside of Salvation Army circles. It's used a great deal by members of the Church of England. They say with some surprise, which rather amuses me, that they had no idea that The Salvation Army might have a sacramental song. Why, I say, indeed all our work is sacramental. It wouldn't be worth doing, were it not so."

This "sacramental song" of The Salvation Army, from the pen of our Poet General, gives eloquent witness that indeed, "God gives songs in the night." At a critical moment, when member nations of the worldwide Army had been ravaged and savaged by war and the miracle of the Army's internationalism hung in the balance, God gave to us this most treasured song that will forever enrich the devotional experience of his people.

For each of his children, however dark the night may be, God comes to the waiting heart with his song of comfort and strength. And like that of the nightingale, the song in the night will be the sweetest strains.

88 Believe Him!
The Holy One Is Waiting

War Time in London

The world's best writing and poetry has come to us from the cauldron of life's strife and struggles. Most of the Psalms were born in a wilderness. Most of the epistles were written in a prison. We can thank Bedford prison for *Pilgrim's Progress.* The golden harvest comes only from furrows that pain has cut.

"Let it be remembered," said the late General Albert Orsborn, "that Salvationists write their songs not in some secluded place, nice and quiet and ideal for meditation. Not at all. They write their songs in the hurly burly of our warfare. I wrote my songs under such circumstances.

"I wrote them during war experiences in London, in the hardest and most difficult of places. I wrote them in my own domestic circumstances surrounded by my children who often crowded around me as I sat at the organ and said, 'Stop writing that song and come and play with us.' In the midst of life and not outside it, these songs were written."

One of the songs Orsborn wrote amid the busyness and warfare of life was "Believe Him! the Holy One is Waiting." In this song, sung to the tune *Adeste Fideles,* he leads us from belief to surrender to full salvation.

> *Believe Him! Believe Him!*
> *The Holy One is waiting*
> *To perfect within you*
> *What grace has begun;*

God wills for His people
  An uttermost salvation;
To sanctify you wholly
  The Spirit will come.

Surrender! Surrender!
  Reject the gift no longer,
But say: Blessed Master,
  Thy will shall be done.
I cease from my striving
  Thy love shall be my conqueror;
To sanctify me wholly,
  Make haste, Lord, and come.

Salvation! Salvation!
  O tell to all the story,
The thraldom of evil
  Is broken and gone!
My sun and my shield,
  The Lord gives grace and glory;
He sanctifies me wholly,
  The Spirit has come.

In the Bible, God's holiness is stressed more than any other attribute. God is portrayed as uniquely and awesomely holy. It is the only attribute thrice repeated: "Holy, holy, holy is the Lord Almighty" (Isa. 6:3; Rev. 4:8).

And wonder of wonders, God invites us to be partakers of his holiness. In fact, he commands us in his word, "As He who called you is holy, you also be holy in all your conduct, because it is written, 'Be holy, for I am holy'" (1 Peter 1:15-16; NKJV). Holiness of heart is not a spiritual luxury for a chosen few but rather the prerequisite for every Christian.

"The Holy One is waiting," is the awesome statement of Albert Orsborn. Divine holiness, moral majesty, sublime splendor wait for us finite and fallen mortals to accept this overture of love and purity. Let us, as invited in this song, believe God, surrender to his will and know the fullness of his salvation.

89 O God, If Still the Holy Place

Renewal in Affliction

"A man in sorrow is in general much nearer God than a man in joy. Gladness may make a man forget his thanksgiving; misery drives him to prayer." So wrote the noted Scottish preacher George MacDonald.

God never wastes suffering in the life of a believer. In life's sorrows comes God's most radiant self-disclosure. He uses trials and testings to strengthen our faith, produce maturity, and build character.

Walking along the rockbound coast of Maine, one observes that the rocks in the quiet coves are rough and sharp, but in those places where the waves beat against them, they are polished. God uses the "waves and billows" of life to polish us.

Albert Orsborn as a young captain in his first corps had a physical setback. He says of that time that "I was rather sick and was thrown into a home of rest to get over my temporary ailments."

During this affliction he found strength and renewal in spending much time in communion with God. From that experience of deepened devotion comes to us his words, "O God, if still the Holy Place is found of those in prayer."

> O God, if still the holy place
>   Is found of those in prayer,
> By all the promises of grace
>   I claim an entrance there.

Give me a self-denying soul,
  Enlarged and unconfined;
Abide within me, and control
  The wanderings of the mind.

Give me the strength of faith that dares
  To die to self each day,
That bravely takes the cross, nor cares
  To find an easier way.

Help me to make more sacrifice,
  To walk where Christ would lead,
That in my life He may arise
  To hallow every deed.

Orsborn describes these words as "a natural outpouring of the soul, a prayer written during my own private devotions."

Prayer is the noblest exercise of the soul, the most exalted use of our faculties, and the nearest approach to God. May we too, whatever our circumstances, claim the promise of prayer as an entrance to God and reach the heights of holiness that he has destined for us.

90 O Love upon a Cross Impaled

Contemplation of the Cross

Commenting upon the writing of his songs, Albert Orsborn closed a taped interview with one he considered among his favorites. He termed it "an Easter song" and said, "Upon his knees before the cross is the place where the guilty sinner comes and it is the place where captains and generals and everybody else must kneel and must stay and finish their course."

From his contemplation on the cross Orsborn wrote the lines, sung to the tune *Mozart*, that may express our devotional response to God's sublime sacrifice for us.

> O Love, upon a cross impaled,
>   My contrite heart is drawn to Thee.
> Are Thine the hands my pride has nailed
>   And Thine the sorrows borne for me
> And such the wounds my sin decrees?
>   I fall in shame upon my knees.
>
> 'Twere not for sinners such as I
>   To gaze upon thy sore distress,
> Or comprehend thy bitter cry
>   Of God-forsaken loneliness.
> I shelter from such agonies
>   Beneath thy cross, upon my knees.

Forgive! Forgive! I hear thee plead;
And me forgive! I instant cry.
For me thy wounds shall intercede,
For me thy prayer shall make reply;
I take the grace that flows from these,
In saving faith, upon my knees.

Now take thy throne, O Crucified,
And be my love-anointed King!
The weapons of my sinful pride
Are broken by thy suffering.
A captive to love's victories,
I yield, I yield upon my knees.

The blood-clotted beams of the cross were once a shame to touch, a "scandal" and "offense" in the words of the apostle Paul. But it was on that cross that love's arms were stretched so wide as to embrace the world. On those crude and cruel beams humankind's spiritual bankruptcy before a holy and just God was wiped out.

From the tragedy of Calvary came the triumph of the Resurrection. The cross has been carved in every form of beauty, worn as a pendant, embossed on our Bibles, emblazoned on the flags of nations, and engraved on the scepters and diadems of kings. By the infinite sacrifice of Christ, beneath its shadow we find life and liberty.

In the last line of each of the four verses of Orsborn's song, the author ends upon his knees. May we, as we contemplate the meaning and the majesty of the cross of Christ, come before it in deepest devotion, upon our knees.

91 Greater Things

From a Time of Discouragement

Albert Orsborn was once a captain in charge of a small corps in England. In his first summer the congregations were swelled with visitors and the full hall encouraged his preaching and ministry.

But when winter arrived in 1908 the summer vacationers were no longer present and the congregation dwindled to a small number. The captain and his lieutenant were discouraged and during their time of morning prayer took their concern to the Lord.

One morning the lieutenant petitioned, "Give us, O Lord, faith for greater things." Those words sparked the tinder of the spirit and imagination of the captain, who went to his desk and penned the song that, with some later revision, has expressed the longing of Salvationists around the world ever since.

What a work the Lord has done
By His saving grace;
Let us praise him, every one,
In his holy place.
He has saved us gloriously,
Led us onward faithfully,
Yet he promised we should see
Even greater things.

Greater things! Greater things!
Give us faith, O Lord, we pray,
Faith for greater things.

Sanctify thy name, O Lord,
By thy people here,
For the altar or the sword,
Save us from our fear.
When the battle rages fast,
Help us in the fiery blast,
Let us not be overcast,
Prove thy greater things.

Every comrade, Lord, we pray,
Thou wilt richly bless;
Lead us forth into the fray,
One in holiness,
One in faith and harmony,
One in perfect charity;
Then we know that we shall see
Even greater things.

Our Lord promised his disciples, "If you believe, you will receive whatever you ask for in prayer" (Matt. 21:22). The apostle Paul affirms the great truth that God "is able to do immeasurably more than all we ask or imagine, according to his power that is at work within us" (Eph. 3:20).

Are results discouraging? Have you toiled with all too little to show for your labor? Do you long to see more fruit for the kingdom? Do you want your life and service to count more for God?

Then pray the prayer of the song that God gave to the young captain in his night of discouragement. God abundantly answered that prayer for Captain Albert Orsborn. Make it your petition. Pray and believe for greater things and prove God's promise and power.

92 Savior, If My Feet Have Faltered

A Sterner Cleansing

A year after Albert Orsborn was appointed divisional commander in South London it was announced that his large division was to be subdivided. He became resentful and rebellious, protesting the plan.

He later acknowledged that as a result of his resentment he had lost his experience of the Holy Spirit's presence and power in his life. During that time, while running for a bus, he slipped and injured his knee. While recovering in an Officers' rest home he heard some of his comrades in a nearby room singing during their prayer time the Army song of devotion: "Nothing from His altar I would keep,/To His cross of suffering I would leap."

He recalled of those moments, "As I yielded, and quietly joined in the song, the tautness of my will relaxed, and I began to be pliant and submissive to the Holy Spirit. Quite frankly, I wept."

Although in distress and spiritual barrenness, God gave him a song in his night that has been a blessing to a countless number. It was first published in 1923 under the title, "The Day That Tries by Fire."

> Savior, if my feet have faltered
> On the pathway of the cross,
> If my purposes have altered
> Or my gold be mixed with dross,
> O forbid me not thy service,

Keep me yet in thy employ,
Pass me through a sterner cleansing
If I may but give thee joy!

All my work is for the Master,
He is all my heart's desire;
O that He may count me faithful
In the day that tries by fire!

Have I worked for hireling wages,
Or as one with vows to keep,
With a heart whose love engages
Life or death, to save the sheep?
All is known to thee, my Master,
All is known, and that is why
I can work and wait the verdict
Of thy kind but searching eye.

I must love thee, love must rule me,
Springing up and flowing forth
From a childlike heart within me,
Or my work is nothing worth.
Love with passion and with patience,
Love with principle and fire,
Love with heart and mind and utterance,
Serving Christ my one desire.

Shortly after the song was introduced, a fellow officer approached Orsborn and said, "I like your songs but please don't say, 'Pass me through a sterner cleansing.' The word 'sterner' is a hard word; why not used instead 'a further cleansing'?"

Orsborn replied, "My friend, you can say 'further' if you like but for me, after what I have been through, it has to be a 'sterner cleansing.'"

If our "feet have faltered on the pathway of the cross," we too may know the Lord's healing and restoration and be counted faithful.

93 I Know Thee Who Thou Art

In the Hour of Bereavement

From the pen of Albert Orsborn, deep from within his soul suffering, comes one of our most beautiful devotional songs. The fourth verse of this song is a favorite in the repertoire of many Salvationists.

I know thee who thou art,
　　And what thy healing name;
For when my fainting heart
　　The burden nigh o'ercame,
I saw thy footprints on my road
Where lately passed the Son of God.

Thy name is joined with mine
　　By every human tie,
And my new name is thine,
　　A child of God am I;
And never more alone, since thou
Art on the road beside me now.

Beside thee as I walk,
　　I will delight in thee,
In sweet communion talk
　　Of all thou art to me;
The beauty of thy face behold
And know thy mercies manifold.

> *Let nothing draw me back*
> *Or turn my heart from thee,*
> *But by the Calvary track*
> *Bring me at last to see*
> *The courts of God, that city fair,*
> *And find my name is written there.*

Orsborn wrote this song in his home in South London in 1942, when severely bereaved by the loss of his wife. He wrote: "I have been permitted to endure extremely heavy and bitter sorrows.

"Once the theme got started, it bore me along, excited and full of praise!" he reflected. "I could not stop it flowing, though the third verse was one 'born out of due time', for it came after the final verse."

The author shared that "the song grew out of my soul under the plowshare of suffering." This inspiring song witnesses that God can bring a golden harvest from the furrows in our lives cut by pain. He gives his song in the night that will resonate throughout our days and bring blessing to others who also travel the path of pain.

Have you experienced a heavy and bitter sorrow? Are you going through a time of trial or suffering? Do you feel almost overcome with a heavy burden?

Then take heart. Look, and you will see the footprints of the Son of God on your pathway. You can be assured that you are a child of God and not alone. You can know his "mercies manifold."

With the Poet General we in renewal would pray that nothing will ever turn our hearts away from our Lord. We also can affirm that we will come at last to the city fair, and find our name is written there. Praise him!

94 Except I Am Moved with Compassion

In the Midst of Poverty and Destitution

The song of General Orsborn that leads us prayerfully to the sacrament of service, perhaps more than any other of his songs, was born in the midst of spiritual poverty and destitution.

Orsborn describes the setting: "In South London in 1923, I saw the barrenness of the situation. I saw churches derelict, all along the south side of the Thames, and hundreds of thousands of the very people we were out to save, wandering without any connection with churches."

From that experience he wrote his song on the sacrament of service.

The Savior of men came to seek and to save
The souls who were lost to the good;
His Spirit was moved for the world which he loved
With the boundless compassion of God.
And still there are fields where the laborers are few,
And still there are souls without bread,
And still eyes that weep where the darkness is deep,
And still straying sheep to be led.

Except I am moved with compassion,
How dwelleth thy Spirit in me?
In word and in deed

234

Burning love is my need;
I know I can find this in thee.

O is not the Christ 'midst the crowd of today
Whose questioning cries do not cease?
And will He not show to the hearts that would know
The things that belong to their peace?
But how shall they hear if the preacher forbear
Or lack in compassionate zeal?
Or how shall hearts move with the Master's own love,
Without his anointing and seal?

It is not with might to establish the right,
Nor yet with the wise to give rest;
The mind cannot show what the heart longs to know
Nor comfort a people distressed.
O Savior of men, touch my spirit again,
And grant that thy servant may be
Intense every day, as I labor and pray,
Both instant and constant for thee.

95 I Have No Claim on Grace

In an Air Raid

Albert Orsborn, who penned some of The Salvation Army's most beautiful devotional songs, relates how he wrote one during a zeppelin war raid.

"This song was written after I had visited a meeting in the East End of London, in the winter of 1916. That, of course, was when war-time London was suffering from zeppelin air raids.

"I had been to a salvation meeting in a little hall in a district called Custom House quite near to the East End docks. There we had a marvelous expression of Salvationism. One's heart was warmed and indeed set on fire by the pure Salvationism of those East End soldiers and converts.

"After this grand meeting where I had listened to so many testimonies and came away with a heart rejoicing, I mounted a London bus, which at that time had an open top deck, to go to my home. After dismounting from the bus I had quite a distance to walk, and while I walked an air raid commenced.

"The zeppelins were overhead, the shrapnel was falling around me on the pavement and knocking up the sparks. Dodging from door to door, I continued on my way with a singing heart and this song formed itself in my mind, on the bus and on the road.

> I have no claim on grace;
>   I have no right to plead;
> I stand before my Maker's face
>   Condemned in thought and deed.
> But since there died a Lamb

Who, guiltless, my guilt bore,
  I lay fast hold on Jesus' name,
And sin is mine no more.

From whence my soul's distress
  But from the hold of sin?
And whence my hope of righteousness
  But from thy grace within?
I speak to thee my need
  And tell my true complaint;
Thou only canst convert indeed
  A sinner to a saint.

O pardon-speaking blood!
  O soul-renewing grace!
Through Christ I know the love of God
  And see the Father's face.
I now set forth thy praise,
  Thy loyal servant I,
And gladly dedicate my days
  My God to glorify.

96 In the Secret of Thy Presence

Between the Hammer and the Anvil

" 'In the Secret of Thy Presence' was the first song I wrote after becoming a divisional commander," writes Albert Orsborn. "In 1920 I did not feel like writing songs. I found myself as a young divisional commander between the hammer and the anvil, the hammer being headquarters and the anvil being the corps.

"I never knew where I was going in my first year and just in the midst of that a request came for me to write a song for the officers' councils. I said, 'Sorry, nothing doing; the song factory is not working.' But finally, on the first night of the councils when I was in my billet, this song came to me quite early in the morning.

"As I sang it over at the piano to my old friend, Lt. Colonel Boot, with whom I was staying at the time, he turned round and said to me, 'Orsborn, that song will live.' It was used that same night in an officers' council and, as they sang this chorus, 'In the secret of Thy presence,' involuntarily, without any suggestion from the platform, they started to rise from their seats until the whole congregation was standing and singing."

> *In the secret of thy presence*
> > *Where the pure in heart may dwell*
> *Are the springs of sacred service*
> > *And a power that none can tell.*
> *There my love must bring its offering,*
> > *There my heart must yield its praise*

And the Lord will come revealing
All the secrets of his ways.

In the secret of thy presence
In the hiding of thy power
Let me love thee, let me serve thee
Every consecrated hour.

More than all my lips may utter,
More shall all I do or bring,
Is the depth of my devotion
To my Savior, Lord and King.
Nothing less will keep me tender;
Nothing less will keep me true;
Nothing less will keep the fragrance
And the bloom on all I do!

Blessed Lord, to see thee truly,
Then to tell as I have seen,
This shall rule my life supremely,
This shall be the sacred gleam.
Sealed again is all the sealing,
Pledged again my willing heart,
First to know thee, then to serve thee,
Then to see thee as thou art.

97 I'll Trust in Thee

In the Eventide of Life

John Lawley (1859–1922) played a prominent role in the early history of The Salvation Army. Following his service as an evangelist, then in corps and divisional appointments, he served as aide-de-camp to the Army Founder, William Booth, for over twenty years and subsequently to General Bramwell Booth. Historian Arch R. Wiggins writes of Lawley's service to William Booth, "Colonel [later Commissioner] John Lawley, his indefatigable A.D.C., was always at his side."

Besides looking after William Booth's personal and official needs, he assisted in his meetings as a soloist and leader of congregational singing. Many souls were ushered into the kingdom during his singing of a prayer chorus or song in the prayer meetings led by William Booth.

Salvationists of those early days often suffered persecution and inhumane treatment at the hands of harsh magistrates. It was not unusual for them to be arrested for alleged obstruction for preaching the gospel in an open-air meeting, to be handcuffed and marched through the streets to prison. John Lawley was among those early warriors. On one occasion he was sent to prison for fourteen days.

Lawley was a noted composer, with eight of his songs in the Army's current *Song Book*. His final composition was written during his last illness when, unable any longer to take up his cherished ministry, he wrote of his unfailing trust in God. That song, given by God in his night season when "no light may shine upon life's rugged way," was sung at his funeral and has been an affirmation of comfort to succeeding generations of God's warriors.

Though thunders roll and darkened be the sky,
I'll trust in thee!
Though joys may fade and prospects droop and die,
I'll trust in thee!
No light may shine upon life's rugged way,
Sufficient is thy grace from day to day.

I'm not outside thy providential care,
I'll trust in thee!
I'll walk by faith thy chosen cross to bear,
I'll trust in thee!
Thy will and wish I know are for the best,
This gives to me abundant peace and rest.

Thy word is sure, thy promise never fails,
I'll trust in thee!
A hiding-place thou art when Hell assails,
I'll trust in thee!
I conquer all while hiding 'neath thy wing,
And in the storm sweet songs of triumph sing.

I'm pressing on towards my home in Heaven,
I'll trust in thee!
Where crowns of life to faithful ones are given,
I'll trust in thee!
This hope is mine, through Jesus crucified,
And all through grace I shall be glorified.

Sooner or later, the sunlit skies over all of our lives will give way to dark clouds and rolling thunder. Health may fail, trials may come, loved ones will be taken from us. But we too may find the Lord's grace sufficient for each day and know the assurance that we are not outside of his providential care. And with John Lawley, faithful warrior of yesteryear, we too may "in the storm sweet songs of triumph sing."

98 No Home on Earth Have I

Amid a Painful Parting

In March 1880, George Scott Railton (1849–1913) led The Salvation Army's "invasion" of America, the first country outside of Britain to become part of this Christian organization that would spread to over one hundred countries. Railton had been William Booth's right-hand man and originator of some of the most brilliant ideas that made The Salvation Army.

In November of that year Railton went to St. Louis to expand the Army's work in the heartland and once again saw great promise for the Army in America. He eagerly looked forward to developing a virile Salvation Army in this land of the free.

However, in January 1881 a communiqué from William Booth brought those hopes to an abrupt end. His orders read for him to return to London. Booth had other needs and plans for this faithful soldier who was closer to him than was anyone outside of his family.

His biographer, Bernard Watson, records: "Railton was shocked and near to insubordination. He felt that his mission had hardly begun. He knew that the conquest of America was only a matter of time; advances had already been considerable. He tried to parley with William Booth."

Railton cabled the founder: "I can come, however it may produce terrible consequences to this Army. The spiritual tide is rising every hour. It is the chance of a generation. Do not let us be short-sighted." But the general, who thought he knew best the needs of his Army, was unmovable and sent a peremptory telegram, "Come along!"

Although disconsolate, Railton packed his bags to return to London, good soldier that he was. His literary bent led him to take up his pen and

242

record his sentiment in verse. It began, "No home on earth have I." This was so literally true of Railton that it became his epitaph. "No Salvation Army verses," writes Watson, "epitomize more closely the life of their writer."

As Railton reflected on this time of uprooting and moving on, he realized that he had only one true dwelling place, as expressed in these lines.

> *No home on earth have I,*
> *No nation owns my soul,*
> *My dwelling place is the Most High,*
> *I'm under his control.*
> *O'er all the earth alike,*
> *My Father's grand domain,*
> *Each land and sea with him alike*
> *O'er all he yet shall reign.*
>
> *No place on earth I own,*
> *No field, no house be mine;*
> *Myself, my all I still disown,*
> *My God, let all be thine.*
> *Into thy gracious hands*
> *My life is ever placed;*
> *To die fulfilling thy commands,*
> *I march with bounding haste.*
>
> *With thee, my God, is home;*
> *With thee is endless joy;*
> *With thee in ceaseless rest I roam;*
> *With thee, can death destroy?*
> *With thee, the east, the west,*
> *The north, the south are one;*
> *The battle's front I love the best,*
> *And yet thy will be done.*

Salvation Army officers closely identify with this song. They are itinerants for God. Their nomadic lifestyle often uproots them after becoming attached to an area and its people. The partings are painful and not always understood.

But in a deeper sense, we are all but pilgrims here on earth. Our true home is with the Lord. As the spiritual puts it, "This world is not my home. I'm just a-passin' through."

Peter addresses the readers of his first epistle as "strangers in the world." Some translations use the words "exile," "pilgrim," "sojourner." Spiritually, we are all sojourners on this planet. In our secularistic society, we need to regain the perspective that we are on a pilgrimage in this short life and our ultimate home is with God.

So if life and circumstance uproot us, and painful partings overtake us, let us take comfort in the affirmation of the Psalmist that the Lord is our true dwelling place (Ps. 90:1). And with George Scott Railton, who became known as "The St. Francis of The Salvation Army," let us say of our soul, "With Thee, my God, is home."

99 I'm in His Hands

An Affirmation during Illness

Stanley E. Ditmer, a former Salvation Army leader in the United States, relates the story behind his writing the song that has brought courage and strength to so many.

"Some 26 years ago I was stationed at the school for officer's training in New York City. I was with a brigade of cadets on a 10-day campaign in April 1956 when I was summoned to Philadelphia, where my brother was seriously ill. It was my task to tell him that he was suffering from lymphatic sarcoma, a type of cancer, and that he would not live more than four months.

"One month later, I too was on a bed of illness. I was confined to the training school, losing weight rapidly. The doctors were unable to diagnose the cause. It was a time of uncertainty and great concern.

"It was during this period that 'I'm in His Hands' was born. It was not 'written,' it simply 'evolved' at the piano keyboard one morning. That same afternoon, I wrote the first verse and the song was laid aside and forgotten.

"Six months later much had changed. My illness had been diagnosed, I was better. My brother was alive and my wife and I were corps officers. We were asked to sing a duet for our annual officers' retreat. The memory of the verse and chorus came to me. I found the copy and wrote what is now the third verse.

"After its introduction, the officers sang the chorus repeatedly. There were many requests for copies, so I wrote another verse and sent it to the Army's *War Cry*, and thus it began its journey around the Army world.

"Although it was born at a time of sickness and death, it was not conceived by me in that manner, but as an expression of virile faith and courage."

> I shall not fear though darkened clouds may gather round me.
>   The God I serve is One Who cares and understands.
> Although the storms I face would threaten to confound me,
>   Of this I am assured — I'm in His hands!
>
> I'm in His hands! I'm in His hands!
> Whate'er the future holds, I'm in His hands.
> The days I cannot see have all been planned for me.
> His way is best, you see — I'm in His hands.
>
> What tho' I cannot know the way that lies before me?
>   I still can trust and freely follow His commands.
> My faith is firm since it is He that watches o'er me.
>   Of this I'm confident — I'm in His hands!
>
> In days gone by my Lord has always proved sufficient.
>   When I have yielded to the law of love's demands.
> Why should I doubt that He would evermore be present,
>   To make His will my own — I'm in His hands!

100 All My Days and All My Hours

In a Chinese Labor Camp

The cultural revolution in China in 1949 forced him to lay down his pen as editor-in-chief of The Salvation Army in China. Confined to a labor camp, he was forced to exchange his pulpit for a pigsty. All on earth that he treasured most had been carried away in the floodtide of change, revolution, and violence.

The stirring saga of Major Hung Shun Yin is chronicled in the historic volume by General Arnold Brown (R), *Yin, The Mountain the Wind Blew Here.* The account relates how, as weary workers trudged homeward at dusk, Yin would fall behind the group and sing The Salvation Army chorus:

> *All my days and all my hours,*
> *All my will and all my powers,*
> *All the passion of my soul,*
> *Not a fragment but the whole*
> *Shall be thine, dear Lord,*
> *Shall be thine, dear Lord.*

His biographer shares that the singing of that chorus became a nightly exercise of worship, an act of devotion. In the semi-darkness at the end of each working day, Major Yin sang in English, softly so as not to be heard, but confident his prayer was reaching God. As months lengthened into years, Yin held his private "divine service." He later testified that the singing of that prayer of consecration kept alive his faith and Salvationism.

247

God had yet another song for Major Hung Shun Yin, a song that would emerge from out of his darkness. In 1981 he came to the United States for the first time. As he walked from the plane into the airport lounge at San Francisco, he heard music of a Salvation Army band. He was greeted by a crowd of smartly uniformed Salvationists, with hands outstretched in welcome.

Then he heard them sing the Army founder's song, "O Boundless Salvation." As much as his taut emotions would allow, he sang with them. He said, "It is 31 years since I heard that song or the music of a Salvation Army band."

Before the huge crowd in Los Angeles he watched and wept as he saw Cadets commissioned and ordained. In the prayer period he was among the first to kneel at the Mercy Seat. He shared with Major Check Yee that he knelt to renew his faith and to pray for his country.

Major Yin's story, of a faith that survived prolonged trial and persecution, eloquently witnesses to the fact that God gives songs in the night.

Acknowledgments

SONGS IN THE NIGHT

Alphabetical Listing of
Songs in the Night

The Author

Colonel Henry Gariepy served for fifteen years as National Editor-in-Chief and Literary Secretary for The Salvation Army prior to his retirement in 1995. He now serves as a National Literary Consultant and has been commissioned to write Volume 8 of the International History of The Salvation Army, covering the period from 1977 to 1993.

He is the author of fifteen books and many published articles. Two of his books have exceeded 150,000 copies, with some going into multiple editions and translations abroad.

The author maintains an active schedule of speaking engagements, including Bible and Writers Conferences. He is an outdoor enthusiast and has finished three twenty-six-mile marathons. He earned his Bachelor of Arts and Master of Science degrees at Cleveland State University and was honored by his alma mater with its 1994 Alumni Leadership Award. He and his wife, Marjorie, take great delight in their four children and twelve grandchildren, all who manifest a love for the Lord.